SIGNS OF THE FALL

SIGNS OF THE FALL

*Understanding and Overcoming
the Seven Deadly Sins*

MATT GORDON

SIGNS OF THE FALL
Understanding and Overcoming the Seven Deadly Sins

Copyright © 2025 by Matt Gordon

Cover Design by Abigael Elliott
Interior Layout and Design by Alice Briggs
Editorial Team: Gin Glass, Donnel McLohon, Kiska Carr, Rhonda Maydwell
Special thanks to B. B. and T. B.

ISBNs:
Ebook: 979-8-89165-241-5
Paperback: 979-8-89165-242-2
Hardcover: 979-8-89165-243-9

Published by:
Streamline Books
Kansas City, MO
streamlinebookspublishing.com

SDG

CONTENTS

INTRODUCTION

EACH YEAR, IT happens. Things are rolling along—trips to the pool, flipflops, long days in the sun. And then it happens. Each year, it does. Fall comes slinking in—abandon all hope, ye who enter here.

What fall means for me is that I'll rake my lawn multiple times a day, every day, for about nine months. Truly, we have this one particularly stubborn tree that holds its bounty of leaves until May. I can almost feel it snickering at me. Babies will be conceived, nurtured along, and birthed, and I'll be out there a-rakin', Quasimodo hunch forming, as I mutter about existence while my back contorts into a suitable question mark.

One year, I recall a singular glorious Saturday. It began in conspiracy, as the neighbors all somehow plotted together and decided to rake their leaves. Afterward, their lawns looked immaculate. However, we didn't get the memo. Our eyesore lawn testified to our exclusion with its knee-high tree litter. And then you know what happened—what beauty transpired? Wind. A lot of it. For four wondrous hours, the air caterwauled at gale-force levels. I half expected Mary Poppins to fly in or Dorothy to soar past. Instead, every single leaf was transported to the lawns of those industrious, foolhardy neighbors. Each leaf served as a message, a reminder, a testament to the utter power of idleness. It was the single greatest day of my life. The next day, I looked out, and my lawn was littered afresh.

I hate fall.

But you know who hates it more—or who would if they were sentient? Leaves. Can you imagine the horror a leaf would be forced to endure each year? Picture it from their perspective: You are just up in your tree throwing shade in the most peaceable possible sense. You are rustling and whatnot, minding your own leaf business, when suddenly, those around you, family and friends, start changing colors. How would you feel if you woke up one day and you were inexplicably yellow? Your spouse is suddenly orange. You've become Bert and Ernie overnight. Then, before you can even deal with this shock, everyone you know turns brown and starts dying. Larry, your neighbor since spring, just falls to the earth one day. This torment would only be exacerbated by the lunatics everywhere, like my wife, who *love* fall.

"Where's Larry?" another leaf friend asks you.

"Down there," you reply. "With *them*."

On the lawn below are children piling corpses and making leaf angels in the bodies. There is a larger human putting dear departed ones—*Is that Larry!?*—in her hair and saying "sweater weather" into a cell phone's camera. Oh, the humanity!

Now imagine a leaf getting carried by some gust to a Hobby Lobby in the autumn months. Talk about morbid. Amid the leaf's shock, it would likely witness my sweatered wife drinking something pumpkin flavored and purchasing nature trash that our backyard provides as a renewable resource for free. "Can't we just go outside and get sticks?" I ask, defeated. Every. Single. Year.

My wife loves fall. She decorates the entire house with acorns. Nuts, indeed. She has this one sign that sits on our porch. It is as tall as I am, and it spells out vertically, from top to bottom, F-A-L-L. That's it! Like someone might be on their way to work and forget what season it is and think, *Oh, I'll drive by that one house over on Dunbar Drive with the declarative decor!* It is like having a sign that says WEDNESDAY or DAYTIME. Or MADNESS.

When autumn rolls in, love it or hate it, the signs of the fall are everywhere. The glow in my wife's eyes, the sis-boom-bah of college football, steaming pumpkin-spice lattes, hayrides, and bonfires. They all declare the season and blind us to two realities of the fall:

1. Winter is coming—cold and colder.
2. It is a season of death—just ask the leaves.

You see, the pleasures of fall distract us from the seasonal suggestion of death. That's good, too. We play and cheer and feast and decorate and snuggle and stoke. After all, these are just seasons—changes in the weather.

But spiritually speaking, the Fall is gravely serious. It is the harbinger of the same things as its seasonal counterpart of the same name. The spiritual Fall means:

1. Winter is coming—cold and colder.
2. Death is in the air.

Similar, too, is that we distract ourselves from this deadly reality. We go on drinking and eating and being merry, yet, truly, tomorrow, we die. Sin assures it.

Well, the cat's out of the bag now—I've said the word: *sin*. Goodbye, dear readers. Just like that, we've thinned the crowd. Our world scoffs at the idea of sin. It is an outdated notion that is as manipulative as it is antiquated. The world mocks sin and says pour one more. Sadly, our churches do too. The church reduces sin to silliness or immaturity;

there's a triviality to it. It's just a phase or a meager escape. It certainly is not that big of a deal. We make a collective truce to neglect it at all costs. *It is harmless*, we lie to ourselves.

The Bible disagrees. Scarcely a page goes by without a declaration against sin. Here are some smatterings of such pages, like leaves falling here, there, and everywhere:

> *Therefore do not let sin reign in your mortal body so that you obey its evil desires. Do not offer any part of yourself to sin as an instrument of wickedness, but rather offer yourselves to God as those who have been brought from death to life; and offer every part of yourself to him as an instrument of righteousness. For sin shall no longer be your master, because you are not under the law, but under grace.*
>
> *What then? Shall we sin because we are not under the law but under grace? By no means! Don't you know that when you offer yourselves to someone as obedient slaves, you are slaves of the one you obey—whether you are slaves to sin, which leads to death, or to obedience, which leads to righteousness?* (Romans 6:12–16)

> *The acts of the flesh are obvious: sexual immorality, impurity and debauchery; idolatry and witchcraft; hatred, discord, jealousy, fits of rage, selfish ambition, dissensions, factions and envy; drunkenness, orgies, and the like. I warn you, as I did before, that those who live like this will not inherit the kingdom of God.* (Galatians 5:19–21)

> *Everyone who sins breaks the law; in fact, sin is lawlessness. But you know that he appeared so that he might take away our sins. And in him is no sin. No one who lives in him*

keeps on sinning. No one who continues to sin has either seen him or known him. (1 John 3:4–6)

If we deliberately keep on sinning after we have received the knowledge of the truth, no sacrifice for sins is left, but only a fearful expectation of judgment and of raging fire that will consume the enemies of God. Anyone who rejected the law of Moses died without mercy on the testimony of two or three witnesses. How much more severely do you think someone deserves to be punished who has trampled the Son of God underfoot, who has treated as an unholy thing the blood of the covenant that sanctified them, and who has insulted the Spirit of grace? (Hebrews 10:26–29)

For the wages of sin is death, but the gift of God is eternal life in Christ Jesus our Lord. (Romans 6:23)

Jesus replied, "Very truly I tell you, everyone who sins is a slave to sin." (John 8:34)

Time and time again, season after season, the Bible puts out a large vertical sign that says, top to bottom: *F-A-L-L*. The evidence of that Fall? It is sin. And the outcome of sin? Death.

The Bible teaches that God—who is love, mind you—hates sin. God hates sin already, and then do you know what sin does? It kills Jesus. About every hymn I was forced to fake sing as a boy made reference to the fact that sin and Jesus's death had a fairly robust causation. And then my children come to mind. Just imagine having a kid. If you already have some kids, just pick your favorite (kidding!). Now, allow your mind to conceive of something greatly harming your precious child. A righteous hatred would be born in you. Let's push the image a bit further—now, imagine folks you love unperturbed or even delighted by the harmful thing that pierced your son or daughter. You see these people laughing about it, reveling in it, or ignoring it entirely. I cannot fathom how sin must make God feel.

I don't have to imagine what it does to me, for the color of my life changes—its wages are death.

Jesus's first and last word to many is "repent" because turning from death is a necessary component of taking up life.

Sin is an action, yes; it is a behavior. But it is also a thought life. A beneath-the-surface paradigm that chooses to believe lies over truth. Sin is like operating from a misguided framework, a bad foundation. It is anti-human. It steals. It kills. It destroys. Yet I fiddle with it like a dizzy toddler with a handgun.

In the beginning, God created the heavens and the earth: form and function, a framework. There is a purpose to seas and skies and how they relate to one another. The same can be said for darkness and light, animals and their habitats, and more. Most of all, there is a purposeful framework to human beings. Tethered to the surface of the earth by an unseen force, given invisible oxygen, provided food from the earth and water from the heavens, humans survive within certain structural realities: form and function, a framework. This plays out in obvious ways in the natural world, and we witness it physically, but spiritually, there is an ecosystem as well. There is God, then us, then all the rest of creation. Within this order, we fit perfectly as subrulers, under God, as stewards of his creation. This order—or way—is the pathway toward a deep peace, a shalom. Shalom speaks of a peace that produces complete flourishing in every fashion. It is living in line with how things ought to be, and shalom is the optimal way of things.

And then comes the Fall.

Humans exchange their birthright for a lie. They trade eternal security for a sinister scheme. Unironically, all that is sinister quite literally begins with sin. The humans sin; they fall, and a new pattern is set, one that operates outside the framework. Augustine says it this way: "In vice there lurks a counterfeit beauty... imitating God but in a perverse way."[1] We, deep down, can feel this too—this tension. We yearn for goodness; we even approach it at times. But we also besmirch it, belittle it, and constantly rebel against it. In short, we just don't quite trust our design nor its Designer, so we take his good framework and try to twist it more to our liking. In so doing, we spoil it. Or, as C. S. Lewis puts it, we allow for the parasite to latch on:

> *The old haunting suspicion—which raises its head in every temptation—that there is something else than God... some kind of delight which he doesn't appreciate or just chooses to forbid, but which would be real delight if only we were allowed to get it. The thing just isn't there. Whatever we desire is what God is trying to give us as quickly as he can, or else a false picture of what he is trying to give us—a false picture which would not attract us for a moment if we saw the real thing... he knows what we want—even in our vilest acts: he is longing to give it to us... only because he has laid up real goods for us to desire are we able to go wrong by searching at them in greedy, misdirected ways. The truth is that evil is not a real thing at all, like God. It is simply good spoiled. That is why I say there can be good without evil, but no evil without good. You know what the biologists mean by a parasite—an animal that lives on another animal. Evil is a parasite. It is there only because good is there for it to spoil and confuse.[2]*

This is what Adam and Eve fell for in Eden. They saw what was and dreamed of what could be, unleashing in their foolishness a nightmarish reality.

After they sin, they hide from God—and all these years later, so do we. Even now, when you choose sin—some mythical mirage of something beyond what God has for you—you lock the door and sin in secret. Our churches are filled with people with plastic smiles, outwardly feigning contentment while sin hollows them from the inside out.

Next, Adam and Eve cast blame. For Adam, it is Eve's fault, and Eve blames the very framework—that God let the serpent enter in the first place. All these years later, we do the same. We will sin, yes, against "stupid" people, people who deserve what is coming. We can rationalize our way from any responsibility. My misdeeds as a husband are always because of the shortcomings of my wife. I'd be the perfect parent but for these unruly children of mine. Just like Eve, we blame God too. If he had just thought it through a bit more, if God really didn't want me to sin, why didn't he give me more pleasures and fewer pains?

Adam and Eve fall. They sin. We fall. We sin.

Shalom is pure. It is good. It is peace, deep and sweet as summer. Shalom exists in the refuge and the shadow of the Prince of Peace—there, we are safe and secure. But we step out from that shadow into the blistering heat of the sun. Rather than return to refuge, we, with waxen wings, take flight, higher and higher, with no need of God or his silly design, his limitations. The pride of our sin lifts us soaring ever upward, and we are the last to see our waxen wings, at such a great height, fatally melting away. Shalom melting with them.

Winter is coming, the death in our lives accumulating like leaves on a forgotten lawn. When the imagery meets reality, the prayer must ascend, "God, we need a rake!" When we rake into sin, here is something we miss sometimes. Jesus didn't die so we could cuss less, drink in moderation, or say more pleases and thank-yous. No, he died to bring us absolute freedom! To drink the cup of poison for us—he downs it. Yet, daily, we take this drained cup in hand and fill it back up, then throw open the hatch. Just think of how Christians discuss sin: *Can I still _____?* or *How much _____ is OK?*

Consider the alcoholic. He comes drinking every day, claiming he can quit drinking any day. And when challenged to quit, he will—tomorrow. He will forsake drinking, save for on the weekends. And Thursdays because they are pretty much weekends. And also Mondays, because, come on, Mondays are tough. And the holidays are coming up, so those are out. And when there are sports on TV because that is way more fun to watch with a cold one in hand.

The questions we ask regarding sin forever focus on how much poison we're still permitted. Sadistically, masochistically, we love death. Poison. Pain. Our own and that of others, for when we sin, it always impacts the lives around us too. I cannot cheat on my wife without hurting my wife.

What if we began shifting the questions to ones like these: *How much freedom can I have? How much peace can I consume? How great a sip from spiritual wonder can I take? How abundant is God?* This is the mindset of Psalm 8:1–9:

> *Lord, our Lord,*
> *how majestic is your name in all the earth!*
> *You have set your glory*
> *in the heavens.*
> *Through the praise of children and infants*
> *you have established a stronghold against your enemies,*
> *to silence the foe and the avenger.*
> *When I consider your heavens,*
> *the work of your fingers,*
> *the moon and the stars,*
> *which you have set in place,*
> *what is mankind that you are mindful of them,*
> *human beings that you care for them?*

You have made them a little lower than the angels
and crowned them with glory and honor.
You made them rulers over the works of your hands;
you put everything under their feet:
all flocks and herds,
and the animals of the wild,
the birds in the sky,
and the fish in the sea,
all that swim the paths of the seas.
Lord, our Lord,
how majestic is your name in all the earth!

We don't need a second-rate, man-made majesty. The provision of God yields freedom and fullness. We think freedom is the ability to choose death when actually it is the invitation to bask in life—to throw off the shackles: It is for freedom you have been set free! To bend the Lewis metaphor, we can go on making snow angels in fields of leafy death, or we can get up and walk to the promised lawn of life.[3]

Jonathan Edwards considers the alternative path for us—the path of death—in his gut-punching sermon "Sinners in the Hands of an Angry God." Our disobedience, our rebellion, is not some child's game. He depicts the sinner walking on slippery terrain, eventually collapsing under his own weight, as no laughing matter.

They are as great heaps of light chaff before the whirlwind;
or large quantities of dry stubble before devouring flames.
We find it easy to tread on and crush a worm that we see
crawling on the earth; so it is easy for us to cut or singe a
slender thread that any thing hangs by: thus easy is it for
God, when he pleases, to cast his enemies down to hell.
What are we, that we should think to stand before him,

at whose rebuke the earth trembles, and before whom the rocks are thrown down?

The wrath of God burns against them, their damnation does not slumber; the pit is prepared, the fire is made ready, the furnace is now hot, ready to receive them; the flames do now rage and glow. The glittering sword is whet, and held over them, and the pit hath opened its mouth under them.

Were it not for the sovereign pleasures of God, the earth would not bear you one moment; for you are a burden to it; the creation groans with you; the creature is made subject to the bondage of your corruption, not willingly; the sun does not willingly shine upon you to give you light to serve sin and Satan; the earth does not willingly yield her increase to satisfy your lusts; nor is it willingly a stage for your wickedness to be acted upon; the air does not willingly serve you for breath to maintain the flame of life in your vitals, while you spend your life in the service of God's enemies.[4]

The author of Hebrews tightens it up a bit: It is a dreadful thing to fall into the hands of the living God (Hebrews 10:31). *Wait? I thought God is love and forgiving and that Jesus wants to take us fishing and all that?* God hates sin. He loathes death. Jesus didn't stay dead, did he? He hates it so much he couldn't give it more than three days to see how it suited him.

Prior to Edwards was a man who was an inspiration to many eventual Puritans, a man called John Owen. If we could reduce this force of a leader down to a phrase, to a tweet, it would be this: the mortification of sin.[5] Believers in Owen's age of yesteryear would war against sin, fighting back the death in their lives. In doing so, they'd more fully taste and see that the Lord is good.[6] Blessed is the person who takes refuge in him and not the things of this world. In clearing out death, they'd create an even greater appetite for life.

Contrary to life is sickness, another thing the fall brings with it. Cold season sniffles in, and you can't breathe properly for a day, then two, then a week. One thinks, *How can this much junk be in my head/face/nose?* We will grab Neti pots and waterboard ourselves—anything to relieve the pressure. After nine or ten days of hacking and sleepless soreness, you wake up, which means you slept! You take a deep breath: clear, easy. *Great is thy faithfulness*, your heart sings.

Spiritually, we walk around congested. We are not fully well—not optimal. We are not as we are meant to be. Rather than do something about it, we just accept it. Over time, we've forgotten that better even exists. That wellness is offered. Soul shalom. Rest.

Sometimes I wonder: *Does anyone even care? Does anyone even want this? Do we ever tire of the feigned spiritual self-help of our day that can deliver us to be 5 percent nicer? Are we weary of settling for a tepid, shallow salvation?*

The call isn't to listen to another TED Talk or read another book that will lead to a smidgeon more happiness in our daily lives. The call is to go to war to liberate a nation, to set captives free, to see the dead raised by putting death to death. That is what fighting sin looks like. That is what I hope you will take from this small book.

During the fall, football season gets going in earnest. If a coach came on television after a loss and said, "Well, we just decided to take the week off on scouting our opponent." That coach would be unemployed by Monday. Christians have an enemy, an opponent. In delving into sin patterns, we catch a glimpse of the enemy's playbook, his tactics, his weak points. And we gain wisdom on how to counterpunch, by the Spirit, toward victory.

An insightful question to ask yourself as we begin this journey is this: "If you were going to destroy you, how would you do it?"[7] Understanding that answer prepares you to trust God's Spirit in the trenches of temptation and to become a liberated overcomer. To have victory over odious addictions great and small in your life. To once more breathe deep, sweet shalom.

This side of heaven, of course, we'll falter, flail, and fall. Of course, we will. And in those moments—as in all moments—grace abounds. But many of us operate with our eyes closed.

Close your eyes now for a second.

It was dark, wasn't it? If the Christian is not considering, confessing, and denying her sin, she is running through life with eyes wide shut.

But as we open our eyes, all becomes clearer. The difference? Light— that's the difference. And, yes, with eyes open, people still fall. Which is why we set forth in community. Together, we see one another and where someone needs to be lifted up, supported, restored. Together, marching forward with eyes open, we avoid pitfalls. Dangers become more obvious.

In this book, I want to challenge you to become a person of the light. The seven deadly sins were originally called the "capital" sins, from the Latin word *caput*, which means "river."[8] From these sins flow all the other sins. Dorothy Sayers writes of these sins that they are "well-heads from which all sinful behavior ultimately springs... the seven roots of sinfulness."[9]

These are the wretched toxins in the poisons we choose or are infected with. They are our sin dispositions. We are going to take a high-level look at each of them, but we won't stop by just realizing how poisoned we are. That would be depressing, and most of us have experienced enough shame in our spiritual lives. Shame culture prevents sinners from taking up their sainthood. We have nothing to hide because God doesn't leave us in our poisoned shame but rather perpetually provides the antidote. He allows us, in Christ, to place death in its grave and dance atop it in victory. Either we come to Christ wanting victory over sin, or we avoid Christ because sin is having victory over us. It is time to turn to the Savior and let him do his thing in our lives.

If I were to have you draw a tree today, I wonder how it would go. Perhaps we are embroiled in a game of Pictionary or something. My guess is that you would draw some roots, a trunk, and some branches. And on those branches? There would be leaves. This is the great tension of life: how it is supposed to be versus how it is not supposed to be.

Fall is a lovely season. Wonders and colors abound. We enter it knowing that it can and will be redeemed. We'll have warmth and friends and make memories. Just as it can be redeemed, so it can be with us. The signs of fall in our own lives can and will be redeemed. We can become a people who heed Jesus and repent, who walk from darkness into increasing light, living in the liberty Jesus purchased for us.

Fall has come—the signs declare it. Let us strive to be trees with leaves on—to be as we ought to be.

SIGNS OF THE FALL

PRIDE

Through pride we are ever deceiving ourselves. But deep down below the surface of the average conscience a still, small voice says to us, something is out of tune.
—Carl Jung

It was pride that changed angels into devils; it is humility that makes men as angels.
—Augustine

I ONCE GUEST PREACHED a series on sin because churches, apparently, just can't find good help. They'd strap a microphone on my head, and I'd get to spend about forty minutes telling a bunch of nice strangers that they are actually wretched sinners. It was a lot of fun. Made a bunch of friends.

Sometimes these wretched sinners would like a chance to respond afterward. Now, in all of human history, not once has someone approached a speaker following a talk to have a conversation without a tremendous amount of awkwardness. The approaching audience member may as well hop up there with their foot already firmly in their mouth. In these tender moments, there tend to be passive-aggressive complaints, non sequitur political insights, rampant oversharing, and, sometimes, downright folly. It has become my favorite part of giving a talk.

But on this occasion, the wheel of time was broken: An elderly gentleman approached and offered kindness, wisdom, and truth. It was a fierce delight,[10] and I was trying to take in each word. This was a difficult task because some bratty kid—some wretched-sinner spawn—was having an absolute meltdown. *Look, control your kid, OK!* I thought, between active-listening head nods and earnest *uh-huhs.* The man kept talking, and the child kept wailing. *Are manners dead? You are in public, you know?* The old guy before me—a picture of perseverance—kept right on. The kid—a portrait of petulance—sought to outlast him. *Would someone muzzle that child!*

Finally, I could take it no more. I had to shoot this kid and his family—wretched sinners the lot of them—a judgmental look. I wanted this look to say, "You should be ashamed of yourselves." I wanted this look to freeze water, to stop time, to spur love and good deeds—or, at least, a time-out or something. So I looked over, grimace firm.

It was my child.

He was absolutely losing it. It was a Hulk-level emotional meltdown there in the church's auditorium. The kind man in front of me kept right on with his own noteworthy sermon, but I suddenly had more pressing matters.

"Excuse me, sir," I interrupted. "That strange chap over there— whom I've absolutely never seen before in my life—seems to be perturbed or, perhaps, possessed. It feels like my Christian duty to attempt to serve him and his noticeably attractive mother."

I approached wondering if doing a sermon on sin was enough qualification to perform an exorcism. In the end, I had to carry the little guy out, kicking and screaming—him externally and me internally. Proverbs 13 says that he who spares the rod hates his son. Well, that is precisely what I did—I spared the rod. My son loves pretzel rods more than Christmas morning, but for three days, he would suffer their loss. He was punished not for having emotions but for wielding them selfishly.

There is more to this encounter than meets the eye. In this episode is a picture of you and me. Each one of us. The Fall happens—sin begetting sin, on down the generational hills the stone rolls. And there is for all of us a first sin. However that sin presents itself, its root is the same. C. S. Lewis calls this sin "the great sin" and "the utmost evil."[11] Others have deemed it the "mother of sin."[12] This particular variety of sin was in the first sin. It was the first sin. And it is the wellspring from which every sin flows. It flows in every heart. When my boy was throwing that tantrum, it was this very sin that raged. Of course it was there in his little mind, body, and soul, he comes by it naturally—he gets it from his father. That sin was in me; it is in me. Let's approach it more carefully than one does a speaker after a sermon. Let's come at it in five acts.

The first act serves as a prelude. It is a flashback. Most of us know about the Fall—that Adam and Eve disobeyed God in the Garden of Eden and ushered sin into the world. But before humankind fell, many biblical commentators interpret another fall. When Adam takes forbidden fruit into his hand, we have this flashback that is also a flashforward, for the age-old sin was born before sin wormed to the heart of mankind. Here is the scene from the book of Isaiah (14:12–14):

> *How you have fallen from heaven,*
> *Morning star, son of the dawn!*
> *You have been cast down to the earth,*

you who once laid low the nations!
You said in your heart,
"I will ascend to the heavens;
I will raise my throne
above the stars of God;
I will sit enthroned on the mount of assembly,
On the utmost heights of Mount Zaphon.
I will ascend above the tops of the clouds;
I will make myself like the Most High."

Traditionally, this scene was thought to depict an angelic being called "Morning Star, Son of the Dawn." Or, for short, Lucifer. We can take much from the passage, but that view suggests two crucial things. First, it reveals motive: that there was a rebellion. This angel sought to be above God, to be "like the Most High." Sound familiar? Second, this passage indicates that this being fell, and, more explicitly, that he had fallen to earth. Here, then, we have the originator of sin, as well as its first salesman. The poison was awakened first in his heart/mind. And what was the exact brand of this destructive force? It was pride.

With this in mind, Proverbs 16:18 becomes both predictive and descriptive: *Pride goes before destruction, a haughty spirit before a fall.* For that first sin in Eden—and for every sin since—that passage becomes literal. It is the very pattern and nature of all sin.

We could get sidetracked here on some logistics. The questions form: *Why was pride, then, even an option? Why did Lucifer even have that choice?* The best answer when we come to big mysterious questions is always and forever this: I don't know. But since I'm writing a book that I want you to keep reading, I'll offer the self-evident answer that is embedded within the diction of the question itself: Why did Lucifer have that *choice*? Why did Adam have that *choice*? Why do we have that *choice*? Well, for the sake of choice. God baked choice into what he created so that love would be real. Without choice, love is a construct. It is the Jedi not choosing good over evil but rather having a certain evolutionary predisposition toward good hard-wired in, which strips the epic from the tale and remakes characters into mere puppets of fate.[13] What makes Obi-Wan heroic is that he *could* be an Anakin. Removing choice from the human is to strip away the humanity from the design of God. And that isn't good at all—it is contrived, forced, domineering. God is love, and from the overflow of that essence we, too, can reflect his nature through our own choice of love. But in that love, God doesn't coerce us. He doesn't bully us. He sets us in favorable environments to realize his goodness. He instructs us. He empowers us. And for God, even rebellion is worth the risk for love. Even to the pain of death, love is worth it—it is the great prerequisite for existence.

Here is a better question for us to ponder: *How did pride work that first time?* That is an immensely valuable question for us because it is foundational. It is what all sin is built on. When a child learns to write, she first attains the alphabet and the sounds of each letter. Armed with such, a six-year-old possesses the same supplies as Shakespeare. Understanding vice and virtue yields us a similar opportunity for poetry to blossom forth from our spiritual lives. Learning to live by the Spirit, choosing to be free, to topple death—this is the foundational knowledge. So, again, how did this first pride manifest?

Well, there in the heart of Lucifer, it came as it always does—it came in like a whisper. A hushed suspicion. This whispered suspicion suggested that perhaps God isn't enough, that God is insufficient, that God isn't supreme or correct or good.

Sin always starts with this suspicion. The whisper grows, finds volume, and then speaks. It begins to like its voice and says it boldly with its chest. Then, before one knows it, it sings it out—shouts it. Through repetition and volume, it tricks us into thinking it is truth. This lie convinces us of its rightness. We feel that justice is on our side and that we deserve something which has been withheld. What happens then? Well, we already know. It is a pattern as old as time.

This pattern is evident in the second act—the past. We saw what came before the beginning, but now we turn our attention to the beginning.

> *Now the serpent was more crafty than any of the wild animals the Lord God had made. He said to the woman, "Did God really say, 'You must not eat from any tree in the garden?'"*[14]

There is that slithering whisper, worming into the heart, infecting the mind, influencing the behaviors, and then hurtling back again from behaviors to mind to heart: a deadly boomerang of destruction.

> *The woman said to the serpent, "We may eat fruit from the trees in the garden, but God did say, 'You must not eat fruit from the tree that is in the middle of the garden, and you must not touch it, or you will die.'"*[15]

Note the subtle unraveling. To our knowledge, what she repeats back, God never said. She added to the command (*you must not touch*). She was basing a growing unbelief on an unset standard. How many of us have broken ties with God based on a thing God has never said? Too many times, we refuse to follow a Jesus who isn't really Jesus at all.

> *"You will not certainly die," the serpent said to the woman. "For God knows that when you eat from it your eyes will be opened, and you will be like God, knowing good and evil."*[16]

The volume of the lie is increasing. And with it, the suspicion increases too. Satan begins with saying that this God guy sounds pretty strange with his weird dietary rules and such. But now we see him twisting the dagger, upping the meds, turning the screw from weird to bad. God goes from majestic to eccentric and then to fabricator, exaggerator, controller, withholder.

> *When the woman saw that the fruit of the tree was good for food and pleasing to the eye, and also desirable for gaining wisdom, she took some and ate it. She also gave some to her husband, who was with her, and he ate it.*[17]

Good and pleasing—sin always appears that way. When Edmund visits the White Witch of Narnia, it is his pride that the prideful hag preys on.[18] She, alone in her haughtiness, turns him against his siblings. And she connects his soul longings to something more visceral—a physical hunger. She allows him to swallow his sin through Turkish delight, a candy he is fond of, and he gobbles from her greedily. She is frozen within and wretched. They say misery loves company. She feeds him her own recipe, and though he eats deeply from her offering, he is never satisfied.

Sin is deceitful like this. Ads for Vegas never show the alleys. Skid row is conveniently edited from reality. What awaits the morning following a night of debauchery never quite comes to mind as dusk dances on. The affair only sees the scintillating Helen of Troy but never grasps the loneliness of a loaded car, driving away from the home of your children following the ravaging divorce.

Sin is good to the eye, while it goes on poisoning our souls, hooking us further and further into its lurid deception. As Lewis said, sin is a parasite. When George Washington fell ill, he was leeched.[19] Yes, this was the way of things then. Face hurts? Stick a leech on it. Broken leg? Let's hurl a leech at it. Maybe not quite that extreme, but it was the medical go-to for his condition. One doctor objected to this treatment for the first president, but the others attending him just kept adding more and more leeches to his emaciated body, eventually killing the man through what turned out to be an unworthy cure. Sin is a nasty bit of leech work that ends in death.

Pride is the pathway of the parasite. First, pride says that God is not enough. That elusive idea of "enough" is found—by me! Wondrous me! I can do better than God through drugs and sex and education and sports and drink and rule keeping and wealth. In something (*anything!*), there is more than God—and I can find it if I pull myself up by my bootstraps hard enough. Second, pride says that I am the master of my fate, the captain of my soul, as the old poem goes.[20] In my freedom—*mine!*—I will keep control. I'm steady. I won't fall down or fall prey. I'm the one that makes it to the top, that avoids the great fall. *Invictus! I am free!*

Early in Genesis 11, we read of some enterprising people who decided to build a city with a tower that reaches into the heavens so that they could make a name for themselves. The Bible mentions that they baked bricks rather than using stone. In other words, they had not just figured out a better way to make better bricks, but also, they believed this achievement proved them better creators than the Creator—quite literally, the sky was the limit for these industrious demi-gods. They dared think themselves equal to God. Theologian Dietrich Bonhoeffer said, "Mankind could point with pride to this fine flower of the human spirit—if it were not for one thing: namely that God is God and grace is grace."[21] How presumptuous to think that man goes to God when, in reality, it is by his grace that God comes to man.

This thinking that we are masters and commanders of our own fates is culturally constructed haughty hogwash. In part, you can see the emperor's woeful nakedness in that this mindset never works! Yes, it produces amazing self-help campaigns. Yes, it is motivational and aspirational. But the reason why something is always aspirational and never consummated is because it is a sham. I stand before a ladder that never ends and dupe myself into thinking that climbing is the way to reach the top. The ladder never ends! Sin is against God, and every good thing is from God. Every breath, every skill, every morsel which sustains, not one is beyond his purview. Which means, at its essence, to sin against God is to sin, too, against ourselves. This is no secret: Scripture declares emphatically that God opposes the proud.

When my son was at church that day kicking and screaming, it was against me, yes. But it was also against himself. When my boys were infants, I'd say to them, with a sing-song cadence, as they kicked and writhed against my changing their diapers, "If you fight me, you will lose." I was being playful with them, but it is true. The day my son threw that fit, I was five times his size. If I had wanted to, I could have hurt him. Or I could have carried him out, past our van, and just put him in the dumpster at the back of the property. As he clawed and yelled against my chest, what he failed to realize is that I am his way home. I clothe him. I feed him. I read him stories and bring order to his life. I am his protection; in me, he moves and breathes and has his being—Christmas gifts and bedtime stories and pretzel rods.

God can do whatever he wants with us. We, in our sin, rage and kick and scream. We need to hear his whisper—allow that voice to pierce our prideful hearts—"If you fight me, you will lose." If we go on fighting him, we lose so very much.

We've seen the prelude of pride and pride in the past. Now we turn to the third act: right here, right now. The present: where you sit reading this book, probably deciding that it isn't for you because you are not prideful. Even now, our pride is at work. Pride can be harder to see in ourselves because, unlike a four-year-old, adults hide their pride-based tantrums. Consider how the book of James says our pride shows itself: "Now listen, you who say, 'Today or tomorrow we will go to this or that city, spend a year there, carry on business and make money'" (James 4:13). You do this very thing, sweet as you are. You have your day planned out. Your week is set. I check my 401K and plan my holidays. I'm the master of my fate. And now what James is going to do is hold your smug face in place, just so, and smack you back to life.

"Why, you do not even know what will happen tomorrow. What is your life? You are a mist that appears for a little while and then vanishes. Instead you ought to say, 'If it is the Lord's will, we will live and do this or that'" (4:14). James says that you don't know what tomorrow holds! He's sort of right, but he is a generous grader because you don't know what's going to happen today. Generally, maybe you'll get close. But if you were to make a minute-by-minute plan for the day, you aren't going to nail it.

I used to do a really mean thing. To quote Hedberg, I still do a really mean thing, but I used to too.[22] The mean thing I used to do occurred when I'd meet with couples for some premarriage counseling. In one session, I'd have them write down separately what they wanted to achieve in their relationship in the first year. Then by year five. Then by year ten. Then by year twenty. Then I'd have them read aloud what they wrote for each section. Oh, you should have seen them! They'd just come to life with dreams of children and white picket fences. Their bodies would get closer and closer to each other.

"Hey, gang, I'm still in here," I'd remind them. "Let's leave some room for the Holy Spirit."

Then I'd take their lists, examine the lists real slow like. And then I'd rip them to shreds—right there in front of them! I'd just tear those loving lists to pieces! While it is good to plan, their plans were woefully inaccurate. Neither of them wrote *infertility* or *cancer* or *child with autism* or *inheritance* or *elder care* or *job loss* or *triplets*—Lord, help them!

James is ripping up our plans before our very faces. He is saying we are mist. We are smoke. Here and gone. Powerless.

In the church that infamous day, my son was *the* master of his fate. He had turned four the week before, and leading up to the birthday, we had showered him with responsibility. When he turned four, he got to play video games, stay up later, pick up for himself, and take his own shower. On Sundays, when I preach, my wife and I take separate cars. That way, if I get canceled, she can get a head start. No, in truth, we arrive at different times, and my son loves going out the backdoor with me. He calls it "the secret way" because kids are awesome like that. They turn dingy backdoors into "secret ways." No wonder Jesus welcomed children. Since I had preached that day, he knew we were going that way. That is what he had planned. He didn't know that his mother had a different plan in mind when she saw I was occupied with an elderly gentleman. He didn't know about that change. All he knew was that he knew best.

Speaking of not knowing, my wife and I didn't know that he had that in him. He's supposed to be our sweet, passive middle child. We didn't know that was going to happen or how to handle it. The people in the room that day—they probably had some ideas. If you see a kid in a restaurant or grocery store, don't you know precisely how to parent them better than the adult who lives with them? We always have the technique or back-in-my-day answer. But you know what we don't know in the restaurant or the store—what those people in that church auditorium that day didn't know? That a child was going to utterly melt down! If they had known it beforehand, we wouldn't be in this mess—or any mess—would we? We'd just get out in front of everything. But we don't know, do we?

Rip. It. Up. We can take all of our pristine plans, all of our pompous certainty about our lives and the lives of others—rip them up. We, all of us, have a young child shouting demands that can flare up any old time, which is basically powerless save for as an illustration in some book. My son's tantrum made it into these pages, but the only

11

place it delivered him that day was to his mother's van. It achieved no secret way, just sound and fury signifying nothing.

James goes on in verse 16: "As it is, you boast in your arrogant schemes. All such boasting is evil." You get what he is saying, right? That our planning and control is rooted in pride. This pride is built upon a suspicion that God is not enough, so we had better step in and do the job.

Having fun yet? I can't believe anyone is still reading at this point. A primary reason for my lack of faith in my beloved readership is that most of you don't think I'm writing to you right now. Think of it like this: Can you think of ten prideful people? I bet you can. Probably with relative ease, too. Now, of the ten people you rattled off, how many of them would suspect they are prideful? One reason they are on your list is because of an unaware arrogance. Pride is a thing so easy to see in others yet that we are blind to in ourselves.

Consider all the ways we boast. We boast of our intellect, our athleticism, our money, our health, our work ethic. This boastfulness forms the ears of our souls, giving that old suspicion a place to whisper. Most of our vanity misses a vital component. I call it Michael Jordan syndrome. In the 1990s people were told to "Be Like Mike." He was the best basketball player on earth (or beyond earth if *Space Jam* was to be believed), and children were reminded of his work ethic. It was Jordan's sheer competitiveness and determination that pushed him toward greatness. Only where did that ethic come from? Well, stories suggest he got it from his mother. He also got food from his parents. It is hard to hoop if you are starving. Further, Jordan grew to be six feet, seven inches with a forty-six-inch vertical. Michael Jordan had an advantage or two in becoming a great basketball player. Now, lest you think I'm trying to take something away from Michael Jordan, I am not. I'm trying to take everything away from Michael Jordan. It is all God's! And that's me talking about a person who is the greatest at something. How much more glaring is it for us common folk who can't dribble left? Every good and perfect thing in my life is from God.

Since the NBA never came calling, I hang my own worth and value on a more everyday facet: parenting. I'm a decent father. I show up. I'm emotionally available. I love my kids and let them know it. And then my son had that moment—the infamous tantrum at church. There he was, yelping and making a scene, and you know what I thought? *I hope people still think I'm good at this. I hope they see me being great at this moment.* In my son's time of dire need, my first thought was of me. God help me. We have nothing apart from God, which is why we are permitted to boast only in the Lord.

Of course, none of this applies to the humble person. Would the humble person please raise his hand? And just like that, the humility is gone. This is the slippery nature of sin. Many of us teeter between boastful arrogance and feigned humility. There's the person who reads about Michael Jordan and says, "Aw, shucks. I'm not good at anything." This, too, is pride. The boastful person craves applause. They are dramatic and self-aggrandizing, always trying to magnify themselves and their accomplishments. They sing it from the rooftops—rooftops they built with their own hands no doubt. But on the flip side is the self-pitying person who lives what John Piper coined "unapplauded pride."[23] They become proud of their invisibility and wear victimhood like a badge of honor. But the truth lies in the middle. God uses you. God gifts you. Taking credit for the gifts is a form of cosmic plagiarism. He designed it and wrote it, yet I stole the royalties and byline. Ignoring the gifts he's given is cosmic neglect or apathy. They are opposite ends of the same sinking ship. It's named the SS *Pride*.

Pride is the black hole of self—wherein the world entirely focuses on you, your desires, your interests, your strengths, your weaknesses, your problems. Eventually, you are the ultimate and only concern. Pride preys on self-centeredness, which is why this inversed common grace insight gets credited to so many thinkers: "Humility is not thinking less of yourself, but thinking of yourself less."

I've always loved reading the journal of George Catlett Marshall. Mostly because it is a short read, as this military marvel, credited with winning World War II, refused to keep a journal for fear it would cause self-centeredness.[24] Now be assured, counselors, I'm not stating that this should be the normative practice for everyone. However, the sentiment of self-forgetfulness must be the heart's position in order to escape pride's grasp and flourish.

We must be careful how we fuel and fan the flame of pride in our lives, for it is a ravenous fire raging within us. Hell is made up of the same fire, a place with nothing to boast of yet which boasts on nonetheless.

Every sin traces back to pride. Cain envies Abel, but at the heart of this envy is the notion that Cain is a better judge of what constitutes a good gift than God is. "God is wrong," says Cain. "I deserve praise." David lusts after Bathsheba. But remember when he does this? Samuel tells us at the opening of that sobering chapter that "it was the time of spring when the kings go to war." What was David's occupation again? Oh, yes: king. Then what was he doing at home? A whisper of pride said, "You are the king. You do so much. For so long. You deserve a rest. You deserve so much." Then when he looked on Bathsheba, the whisper turned full-throated, "You deserve this." The spring of pride yields a garden of death.

Historically, pride comes before the fall. Alexander the Great only trusted the greatness of himself, and it cost him everything. Napoleon trusted his own genius to know there was no point in packing for winter, and his army (and ambitions) froze. William Henry Harrison needed to live up to his reputation as a hardened leader, so he didn't wear a coat to his inauguration. He died weeks later from pneumonia.

Pride is every church you see that abandons its first love for the love of self, size, and systems. The fall is coming.

Parse a sin down, like a sentence, and the essential verb is that old, sneaky whisper that God is not enough. We are sick with it. The forbidden fruit has poisoned us as a world, as a church, and as a people. We desperately need a cure.

The sickness was born in the prelude, infected the past, and challenges the present, but there is a prescription offered in act 4. The antidote, pride's antithesis, is humility. God resists the proud, but he gives grace to the humble; he blesses them. In our weakness, there is strength. Think of the church—its head is Christ, and its body is made up of many parts. Not one super great part. Not some very talented pastor-CEO part who can sing and pray and dance and sway. No, many parts. That means we all need each other and we are all lacking. We all have screaming children in our lives in some form or fashion. When I hear someone talk about a "proud church," it is an oxymoron and surely moronic. A humble church is a group of people who don't know everything—but have the answer. A humble church is a group of people who listen and learn. A humble church is a group of people who help one another because, but for the grace of God, there go I. A humble church doesn't go around touting, "I pity the fool." A humble church is a group of people wise enough to declare, "I *am* the fool. Help me, Jesus."

Humility is the great prescription doled out by that great physician. The seven deadly sins tremble at the presence of the leader of the capital virtues. Saint Augustine once gave students three pieces of life advice that went as follows: "The first part is humility; the second, humility; the third, humility: and this I would continue to repeat as often as you might ask for direction."[25] Humility is the antidote to pride. But how does one take this sacred medicine?

We began this chapter with a flashback to the originator of sin/ pride, and now we turn to the last of five acts—the prevailing, the origination of pride's unmaking, its counteraction. And here we find a bookend. It was Adam—the sinner—who reached for what was forbidden. He was the first man. The first Adam. Pride is often called the "Mother of Sin." This familial language takes my mind out to the ballpark. A once-great pitcher named Pedro Martinez dominated the sport but could not solve the Yankees—the Yankees would make this ace routinely look like a chump on the mound. In the playoffs, Yankees fans would serenade the struggling hurler with chants of "Who's your daddy?" They said it over and over and over again. This is the chant that calls out to every Christian. Its answer determines which voice we follow: the Serpent's suspicious whisper or the Lion's tender trusting purr.

In truth, Adam is my father. My heredity traces back. Eventually, some overpriced genetic test would wind its way back to him. If my father were a serial killer, and as a boy, I began torturing rabbits, people would say that I look a bit like my father. I have him in me. So, when it comes to pride, yeah, I come by it naturally. I come from Adam. Chalk it up to bad genetics.

In the biblical curse, after Adam sins, God says that he will return to dust.[26] This is where we get the line "from dust to dust." Much later, when Jesus is talking about entering his family, he tells Nicodemus (John 3) that he must be "born again." To be born again means many things, but one thing it promises is new parentage. New heredity. New genetics. A new father.

And this father is not from dust. The Second Adam was placed in a womb, a wellspring of life, a new man offering an altogether new way. He walked the same old pattern too. Look at Matthew 4:1–9:

> *Then Jesus was led by the Spirit into the wilderness to be tempted by the devil. After fasting forty days and*

forty nights, he was hungry. The tempter came to him and said, "If you are the Son of God, tell these stones to become bread."

Jesus answered, "It is written: 'Man shall not live on bread alone, but on every word that comes from the mouth of God.'"

Then the devil took him to the holy city and had him stand on the highest point of the temple. "If you are the Son of God," he said, "throw yourself down. For it is written:

"He will command his angels concerning you,

And they will lift you up in their hands,

so that you will not strike your foot against a stone."

Jesus answered him, "It is also written: 'Do not put the Lord your God to the test.'"

Again, the devil took him to a very high mountain and showed him all the kingdoms of the world and their splendor. "All this I will give you," he said, "if you will bow down and worship me."

Jesus is repeatedly offered the same deal as Adam: Deny the Spirit. Distrust God. *Surely, God doesn't want you to be hungry. Surely, God has to prove his power. Surely, God doesn't have dominion here.* Jesus gives his answer to these temptations, to the gambits of pride, in Matthew 4:10–11: "Jesus said to him, 'Away from me, Satan! For it is written: "Worship the Lord your God, and serve him only."' Then the devil left him, and angels came and attended him."

Satan comes with the same tired strategy. Why change it out? It had never failed. When he approached Adam in paradise, Adam was a fully satiated man. He whispered suspicion, and the man ate the temptation of pride. With Jesus, it is the wilderness, and the man is empty. Starving. Satan whispered the suspicion, and yet pride is denied. God is trusted.

Jesus had the notes; he'd written them. Love casts out pride. The older virtue superseded; there was a secret way. The host consumed the parasite. Jesus had the humility to face hunger—for God's Word is nourishment enough. He had the humility to drink the cup of wrath—for God's will be done. Jesus had the humility to be raised to life—for God's life is abundant.

Jesus was stripped, mocked, and hung on a tree. That first rule, that first sin, centered on a tree. Its fruit was pleasing to the eye. That first foundation, that first virtue, centered on a tree, its fruit made wretched as sin, a bloody eyesore.

The first tree and its fruit brought poison. The second tree and its fruit brings life eternal.

This fruit is offered daily to the lowly. To the sick. To those who approach that tree, to those who abandon temper-tantrum suspicions and trust the Second Adam. Where pride grows, the cross shrinks, and the Savior with it.

I don't need help.

I'm not that bad.

I've got a plan.

Thank goodness I'm not like...

When our humility grows, we see our sinfulness, the cross grows, and the Savior does too. We call out, "Woe is me," and are met with a tender answer: "Blessed are you."

Jesus came not to alter behaviors but to change our family. New birth, new heredity, new genetics. He changes out our stone hearts with ones made of flesh.

The first Adam sought vision by shutting his eyes. He ran to the desert depths in search of water. He was a moth contending the flames. The dry leaves of fall opposing an all-consuming fire. A small child raging against his father.

The Second Adam opens eyes with light. He quenches thirst with living water, carries the weight, and washes our feet. In him, I am adopted, cherished, provided for, and taken safely home. In laying himself down, I am lifted high. So again comes the question: Who's your daddy? Is it the first Adam or the Second? Each moment of each day, I'm asked which father I choose. Which tree, which master, do I bow before? In that choice, I am cast to the dust in pride or, in humility, birthed to blessed life.

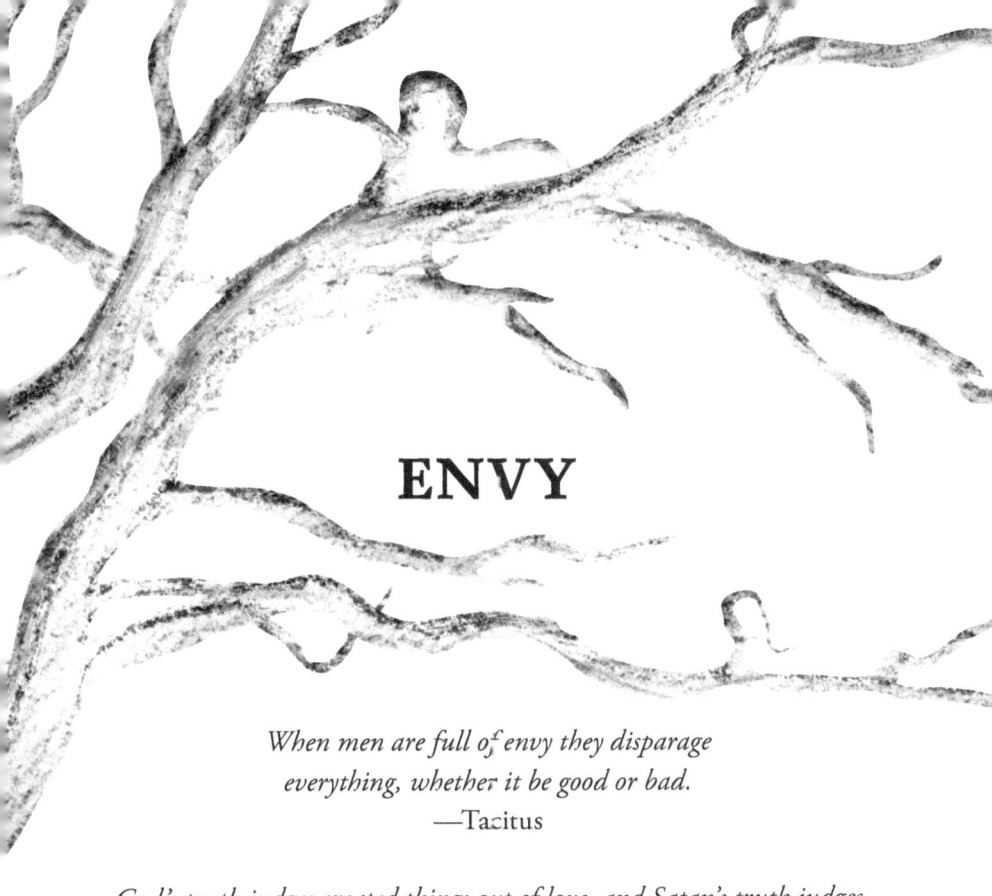

ENVY

When men are full of envy they disparage
everything, whether it be good or bad.
—Tacitus

God's truth judges created things out of love, and Satan's truth judges
them out of envy and hatred.
—Dietrich Bonhoeffer

SOMETIMES I GET invited to things. Startling, I know. At one such event, there were assigned seats for dinner. Each spot had a little name card indicating where folks should sit. The nice part about this is that it prevents the Forrest Gump bus situation. Remember when Forrest was on the school bus and no one wanted him to sit with them? Imagine doing that dance with a plate of roast beef. Despite the advantage of assigned seating, there are negatives to this arrangement too. One of these is another Forrest

Gump-ism: "You never know what you're gonna get." In *Curb Your Enthusiasm,* Larry David has a whole episode about the importance of a good "middler" at a dinner party. This is the person who sits in the middle seat of a table and helps keep everyone engaged in stimulating conversation. When your table is assigned, it could lack a middler, displace the middler to the far reaches of the table, or have an entire table of middlers, which would cause an overwhelming eruption of extroversion.

Another negative that becomes evident from assigning seats is comparison (which is usually the birthplace of envy). You'll be sitting there at your table listening to the nonmiddler bore the entire table with a too-long account of the perceived flaws in the electoral college or his decision-making process in fantasy sports drafts when your gaze lifts. You go from looking at his vacant eyes to staring longingly at nearby tables. One collection of folks is laughing uproariously—oh, to chew the fat with them! Another table is pensive, reflective—*their freaking lives are changing over at table nine, and I'm over here listening to people one-up each other about their gout flare-ups.*

There are good dinner mates and bad ones. And then there are some that would be so good that they'd become bad. *If I have to hear "Confucious says" one more time, I'm gonna lose it. All I asked him was to pass the salt!* Aesop would be in this same camp as Confucious. He would be a charming dinner mate at first, with his tidy stories and tidier morals. But then he'd go from your table and get all up in your kitchen like he did when I read his story entitled "Avarice and Envy."

In this tale, these two characters stand before a god and demand that this god give them each their heart's desire. The god agrees but adds the caveat that whatever the man wished for would be doubled for the other man. The first guy is greedy, and he wishes for treasure. So he is given treasure. However, the second man gets double the treasure. The second man thinks about this then, in his envy, wishes to be blind in one eye.[27]

Another Greek, Socrates, called envy the "ulcer of the soul."[28] But maybe this all sounds Greek to you? Aesop is famous for writing fables, after all, not nonfiction that matches our modern experience. Lest you think envy has expired, consider some not-so-ancient behavioral economics findings. In one study, for instance, respondents were asked if they'd prefer a situation in which they would make $50,000 a year while all their close friends and relatives made $25,000 a year or make $100,000 a year while all their close friends and relatives make $250,000. In these scenarios, there would be no cost-of-living differences—it is just the difference between your earnings in each scenario. Which would you choose? Now, I'm no finance guy, but I can tell you this with certainty: $100,000 is more money than $50,000. Yep, did that math in my head too. The other thing I can tell you is that most people, if given a choice, would choose more money over less money. But in this test, they don't. The majority of people would rather make half as much in order to outearn those around them.[29]

A similar test was done in which respondents chose between the following situations:

  A. You are the 100,000th person to buy a ticket at a movie theater and are thus gifted with a $100 gift card.
  B. The millionth person to buy a ticket is in front of you in line. For being the millionth customer, they receive $1,000, and you get $150 for being next in line.

Which one do you choose? If you are like the majority of the participants in the research study, you choose option A, a decrease of $50![30] Forget the large popcorn and slushy. You'd rather have a bucket of misery.

Or take the well-known Ultimatum Game.[31] Versions of this have been used on gameshows for decades. Its traditional form features pairs of people dividing $100. Partner A proposes a split. If you agree, you each get the proposed amount of cash. If you don't agree, neither of you gets a thing. Now, if you are a logical participant in this game, you know what your answer ought to be to any proposed deal: *Yes!* Eighty–twenty, yes. Seventy–thirty, yes. Even ninety-nine–one, yes. That represents one more dollar than you would otherwise have, which is, you know, one more dollar than you would otherwise have! However, most offers that come in with worse payouts than seventy–thirty get rejected. The reason for the rejection? It's obvious: It isn't fair. A sentiment that is the birth notion of envy. It happens with money, circumstances, and even assigned seating. Unfairness produces envy, or, more accurately, our perception of fairness in relation to our perception of self produces envy.

As stated last chapter, pride is the mother sin. You just can't find a sin without it, because without pride, you are left with humility and submission. Psychologists and philosophers call this "incompatible action."[32] I cannot stand and sit at the same time—the actions are incompatible. If I humble myself and submit to God, I cannot, at the same time, pridefully rebel against him.

Pride is the distortion of reality that says I am smarter, richer, wiser, more judicious than God and others. Envy, then, is reality's stark rebuttal. I cannot be the richest person in the room when Elon Musk strolls in. Reality smacks me in the face, and that rich man (and the God behind the scheme) becomes the one keeping me from my deserved place. I cannot be the smartest in the room when Bill Gates shows up. I cannot be the most attractive in the room, well, ever. And *That's not fair*, my heart wails.

Dorothy Sayers says, "Envy hates to see other men happy. It is a great leveler. Where it cannot level up, it levels down. At its best it is a climber and a snob. At its worst, it is a destroyer."[33] Aristotle describes it as a "disturbing pain excited by the prosperity of others."[34] Frederick Buechner writes that envy is the "consuming desire to have everybody else as unsuccessful as you are."[35] Envy can be benign or malicious. The benign type is a personal misery that leads to inaction or the mimicry of the enviable person. The malicious type is active and seeks destruction, pain, and comeuppance for the object of envy. Neither type sounds much like happiness and even less like Jesus.

Envy is readily (and sometimes initially) experienced between siblings. For the only children reading this book, let me give you a glimpse of how siblings operate via the hypothetical example of two young brothers, named with total randomness (that has nothing to do with my own sons, M. J. and Joseph), say, R. J. and Yoseph, and now we place a single cookie between them and observe:

R. J.: *Oh, please, give this last cookie to this kindly gentleman across from me.*

Yoseph: *No, no, no. I couldn't possibly. Let us share it evenly at the least, or, at most, give me a double portion of honor by bestowing my half to this esteemed personage, R. J.*

R. J.: *Brother, your love for me is sweet enough for a cookie-less lifetime.*

And so it goes—*never*! That sugary scene ends in claw marks and tearstains—there will be blood! Freud is credited with the term "sibling rivalry," but we've known it since time began.[36] There are only so many cookies—kindness and power and love—to go around. So we compare, count, and control. We also envy, envy, envy.

Now think of sibling rivalry and the familial language of the Bible. We have God the Father, and in Christ, we are made siblings. We hate each other because we treat God with a scarcity mindset. If my brother takes the cookie of God's love, what if there isn't enough for me?

Proverbs 14:30 says, "A heart at peace gives life to the body, but envy rots the bones." This imagery of bones rotting makes me think of the liters of soda I drink every day. A little old woman went viral once because she was super old. She had a high quality of life despite her age, so the news went to do a story on her. She claimed that her key to vitality was drinking five Dr Peppers a day. A couple doctors had told her to quit, and she had outlived both.

I like the story, but I know she is probably wrong. Soda is bad for my teeth and my bones. It doesn't make me faster or stronger. Of course, it never claims to. I've never seen Dr Pepper market its long-lasting health benefits. It makes no promises. In truth, all it does is kill.

Envy is like that. All the other sins promise something. They even deliver in part and for a time. That is why they are such effective seducers. "Of all the seven deadly sins, only envy is no fun at all," writes Richard Epstein.[37] Sins are like slot machines, giving these small payouts that rob us little by little over time. The promise of an occasional jackpot operates like a drug. Pride says we'll be on top. Anger cackles for revenge. Greed promises wealth. Sloth sends brochures depicting ease. Lust dances in with pleasure and control. Gluttony serves up pleasure and comfort. Envy, though? All it says on the can is that it brings misery and resentment. Yet we tilt our heads back and binge the stuff.

Satan's pride sought to make him higher than God. In punishment, he was cast down to earth. Once there, he parts the bushes and sees a table with assigned seating. There is a place for God and for man and for woman. But there is no place at that table for him, not without humbling himself, which is an incompatible action for the manifestation of pride. So, Satan does what Satan has always done—he begins a mission. This first mission looks like all the rest: Steal. Kill. Destroy. That devilish MO is laid out in John 10:10: "The thief comes to steal, kill, and destroy." And what is the thief after in this first foray? Dignity. Here—and since—humankind is made in the image of God. An image Lucifer tried to co-opt but couldn't have. And this is an earmark of envy and is echoed in the behavioral studies referenced earlier: If he can't have it, he'd prefer that no one does. He attacked because he envied. Here is a more puritanical take on it from Jonathan Edwards:

> *The Christian scheme of doctrine teaches us how Christ came into the world to deliver us from the fruits of Satan's envy towards us. For the devil, being miserable himself, envied*

> *mankind that happiness which they had, and could not*
> *bear to see our first parents in their happy state in Eden,*
> *and therefore exerted himself to the utmost to ruin them,*
> *and accomplished it. The gospel teaches how Christ came*
> *into the world to destroy the works of the devil, and deliver*
> *us from that misery into which his envy had brought us.*[38]

Let's look at a few other biblical scenes of envy.

> *"Very truly I tell you, when you were younger you dressed*
> *yourself and went where you wanted; but when you are old*
> *you will stretch out your hands, and someone else will dress*
> *you and lead you where you do not want to go." Jesus said this*
> *to indicate the kind of death by which Peter would glorify*
> *God. Then he said to him, "Follow me!"* (John 21:18–19)

Jesus gives this prediction above and Peter doesn't respond with "Cool" or "Sounds good" or "Can I ask a follow-up or two?" No, envy bubbles forth.

> *Peter turned and saw that the disciple whom Jesus loved*
> *was following them. (This was the one who had leaned*
> *back against Jesus at the supper and had said, "Lord, who*
> *is going to betray you?") When Peter saw him, he asked,*
> *"Lord, what about him?"*

Here, Jesus tells Peter a thing, but rather than receive that thing, Peter has to make sure that someone else doesn't receive something better than him. In our world, this is like meeting trials in your life with, "What about Yoseph? Why isn't he sick/poor/unemployed/ etc.?" Notice, too, the details thrown in about the way John ("the disciple whom Jesus loved") was treated and seated at the supper.

Think Peter hadn't noticed? Peter had been keeping score. Are you constantly keeping score?

Another famous bout of envy comes from Israel's first king. This shows that a person doesn't get promoted above the lure of envy. No job title or tax bracket shelters you from this madness. The following passage is 1 Samuel 18:5–9:

> *Whatever mission Saul sent him on, David was so successful that Saul gave him a high rank in the army. This pleased all the troops, and Saul's officers as well.*
>
> *When the men were returning home after David had killed the Philistine, the women came out from all the towns of Israel to meet King Saul with singing and dancing, with joyful songs and with timbrels of lyres. As they danced, they sang:*
>
> *"Saul has slain his thousands, and David his tens of thousands."*
>
> *Saul was very angry; this refrain displeased him greatly. "They have credited David with tens of thousands," he thought, "but me with only thousands. What more can he get but the kingdom?" And from that time on Saul kept a close eye on David.*

This is like *The Office* basketball game. Dwight steals the ball from his teammate, leaving a flummoxed Ryan to call out, "Same team, Dwight!"[39] Saul is at war against the Philistines. David is at war against the Philistines. Saul can dislike all sorts of things about David—his height, if he smells like sheep, his musical sensibilities. Still, the enemy of my enemy is my friend. David is defeating Israel's foes. For Saul, this is a good thing. Furthermore, Saul has his envy ratcheted up by a song. These women don't know David killed ten thousand Philistines. In fact, they likely know he didn't. It is a song, not a fact. This all showcases another thing about envy: It is often absurd. Logic had left the building. Saul had the pride of a king, and it created a royal envy. We follow this same pattern when we want comeuppance for folks. When we have to keep our eye on them. When we fixate on them. When their successes agitate us.

Take the story of Cain. Notice how envy drives him to murder:

> *In the course of time Cain brought some of the fruits of the soil as an offering to the Lord. And Abel also brought an offering—fat portions from some of the firstborn of his flock. The Lord looked with favor on Abel and his offering, but on Cain and his offering he did not look with favor. So Cain was very angry, and his face was downcast.*
>
> *Then the Lord said to Cain, "Why are you angry? Why is your face downcast? If you do what is right, will you not be accepted? But if you do not do what is right, sin is crouching at your door; it desires to have you, but you must rule over it."*
>
> *Now Cain said to his brother Abel, "Let's go out to the field." While they were in the field, Cain attacked his brother Abel and killed him.* (Genesis 4:3–8)

Cain is too proud to change. God clearly challenges him to do right, but repentance is the more difficult path. Rather than play by the rules of existence, Cain took his ball and went home. Can you imagine him, too, festering with this envy? He muttered alone, his envy working up an anger: *This is not fair.* Pride led to envy, and that envy spawned resentment, loathing, and eventual violence. This is how malicious envy always plays out—with destruction.

When I read about envy, I think about a friend and how I wish he wouldn't be so dang envious. Or my neighbor. Or a sibling. Or a coworker. I can name envious people for days, poor souls. And in making my list and checking it twice, I rob myself of the gift of conviction concerning my own envious heart.

This one time, I broke my wrist. I knew it was broken because, well, it was broken. My wrist had always been a certain way, and then I fell during a soccer game, and it was a way it had never been. It hurt, and I felt sick. But my dad thought I could sleep it off. He wasn't certain it was broken. The next day, it felt just as broken as the day before. My dad had grown up playing rugby, and I think he would have given it another month or two. Fortunately, my mother returned from a trip and rushed me to the doctor.

Mark 2:17 says, "On hearing this, Jesus said to them, 'It is not the healthy who need a doctor, but the sick. I have not come to call the righteous, but sinners.'" We need a physician. All of us do. But many of us are content to hobble around and save face with broken-down bodies. When we are accursed with malady, we must be carried and laid at the feet of the most skilled doctor. Jesus is waiting to heal us, to treat us. But we have to raise our broken arms for assistance. Perhaps, too, we need to check the symptoms—and not of our spouse or neighbor or coworker. We need to look at our heart and test it for signs of the fall. Where might envy be twisting our souls and rotting our bones?

One obvious symptom of envy is comparison. We find ourselves in destructive patterns of fixating on how much money someone else makes, how great their life is, how wonderful their trips are, how they look, or who they're with. Online, we doom scroll. Scholars have begun using the term *Facebook envy* to capture the negative effects on well-being prompted by the envy-inducing way we utilize social media.[40] One psychologist has labeled our society as an "other-directed culture."[41] What this means is that what is good and valuable is dictated not by goodness and value but rather solely by what other people have. We, hence, follow a made-up standard and chase futile dreams that have us longing for stuff we wouldn't even truly want if envy hadn't blinded us to truth. This unfulfilling cycle creates an insatiable madness.

One answer to the disease of comparison is true community. A thing happens when you get to know the people you might otherwise envy. It's this: You know them! In knowing them, you will see their desires, their wounds, their trials. An old maxim says that the cure for falling in love with someone is to get to know them. Indeed, how many of our marriages would persevere through the darkest times without a vow! No, it is the very vow—one that acknowledges both sickness and health that allows the perspective necessary to persevere. When you know people really well, you know, too, that they are people. A tactic of envy, though, is to isolate. To sever community. We witness this daily in our polarized culture. We cut people from our lives who are richer than us or poorer than us or who vote differently than us, thus further distancing ourselves from others and inviting us to only see the bits of them we want to see or they want us to see.

Comparison is sneaky too. Sometimes, it can be masked by the person just trying to offer a "helpful critique" or claiming the title of "truth teller." But, if we are honest, our verbal putdowns and subtle eye rolls have little truth in them—it is just envy throwing a pity party.

Complaining, too, is another form of comparative envy. We complain on the basis that better gifts exist and have been withheld. Which gifts? Well, obviously, it is the one someone else possesses that is proximate to us. I write things down and say things for much of my living. Sometimes, I watch TV shows and see people flying in helicopters. I feel no pangs of envy, nor do I find myself wishing that I had a helicopter of my own. There are people who probably do have envy about the helicopters of others—they just don't live in my zip code. No, I find myself envious of other people who write things and say things. *Their prose is lacking* or *Their sermon too long*, I'll critique.

When this sort of spirit arises, here are two helpful questions: Is God good or not? Are good gifts all from him? If I say yes to both of these, it means that God is good and all gifts are from him—my own gifts and the gifts of others. I need to trust him.

We need to trust him. Envy is not a secular problem that somehow vanishes once someone pulls into a church parking lot. In fact, I have a scheme to destroy the local church based on envy. Now, the church will prevail—so my little scheme wouldn't eradicate Jesus's Bride or anything. But I could take down a bunch of churches in my town if I wanted to and if they aren't walking in wise humility. It wouldn't be by putting laxatives in their coffee or disrupting their services. No vandalism would be necessary in this plan. In fact, I wouldn't even need to break the law. Here is what I would do: I'd start a blog. Then, on that blog, I'd put out a weekly ranking every Tuesday on the sermons for the week from the various local churches. Each talk would have a title and the pastor/speaker who gave it, and I'd just rank them. There'd be a top-ten ring and other hollow, flashy stats. And you know what would happen? A pastor would look. And he'd get mad that the guy from Third Baptist was ahead of him. So that week, he'd do whatever he could to top that guy. Then he'd check the following week, and he'd feel good because the guy from Third Baptist fell out of the rankings due to an untimely talk on giving, but the chump from Second Baptist took his spot! He doesn't even want to think about where they ranked the fellow—you know, the one with the fancy PhD and even fancier car—from First Baptist. I'm telling you, pastors would lose their first love so fast, or at least have that true first love revealed. In truth, most of us only need a mirror to see our true first love. Congregations would lobby for their pastors and smear other pastors. It would be a disaster. All unleashed by unguarded hearts and the sinister trespass of envy.

And envy is ever-present. We can find envy even in "good" things. There are good forms of activism—when a person sees a need and sacrifices to try to see that need met for others. This is beautiful and necessary in a broken world. But there is bad activism too. The appearance is righteous, of course—Satan masquerades as an angel of light, after all. This bad kind doesn't take up arms to right injustice. It takes for the sake of taking—it takes for the sake of envy. Many people who want to topple the king, scapegoat the queen, railroad the pastor, expose the friend, aren't actually interested as much in a dethroning, but rather a self-coronation. I whisper slander about my boss because in my mind, in the quiet recesses of the night, I am sat in his chair, sipping contentedly from a "World's Best Boss" mug. Beware passive-aggressive action in your life—our hearts can be factories of self-deception.

Another symptom of envy is its lurid consumption. Think again of Saul or Cain. Envy begins as a quiet resentment, then comes cloaked contempt. Eventually, open disdain enters, then hatred. That hatred simmers, boils over, and violence/removal is the only way to appease obsessive longing. We can't let envy go, and then, given time, it won't let us go—it has a stranglehold on our hearts. When you assess your own gifts, are you appreciative, content, and driven to develop them and invest your varied blessings into multiplied future blessings for the world around you? More likely, you assess your own lot in life and are consumed by ingratitude. Consumed by your private enemy who has what should be yours. Consumed by your designs to take what you rightfully deserve. Consumed by discontent. Envy casts you adrift in a sea of your own making; you are made salty as that vast, dark water that overwhelms your existence.

And then there's Peter. I mentioned his moment of envy in John 21:21. Now, listen to him later in life:

> *Therefore, rid yourselves of all malice and all deceit, hypocrisy, envy, and slander of every kind. Like newborn babies, crave pure spiritual milk, so that by it you may grow up in your salvation, now that you have tasted that the Lord is good.* (1 Peter 2:1–3)

He instructs people to "rid" themselves of envy. If he didn't think it was possible, he wouldn't say it. If my high school basketball coach had just yelled, "Dunk it!" at me over and over again, I would have quit the team. *Bro, have you seen me? I can't dunk with a stepladder.* Peter is telling us to rid ourselves of evil because this is one of those things that fits under the umbrella of "possible" with God. It's a pretty big umbrella.

Here's another scene of Peter—and stay with me: We're doing a thing here, I promise!

> *The priests and the captain of the temple guard and Sadducees came up to Peter and John while they were speaking to the people. They were greatly disturbed because the apostles were teaching the people, proclaiming in Jesus the resurrection of the dead. They seized Peter and John and, because it was evening, they put them in jail until the next day. But many who heard the message believed; so the number of men who believed grew to about five thousand.* (Acts 4:1–4)

I don't need to explain to you what happened here, right? Peter gets arrested. He gets jailed. He then gets a stern talking to and told not to share about Jesus anymore. He says no. Wait? None of that is actually right. Here is how it really went: *They* get arrested. *They* get jailed. *They* get a stern talking to and told not to talk about Jesus anymore. *They*. It isn't just Peter, is it? It is Peter and *John*. John! That is the guy that Peter was envious of back in John 21! Something is different, but how?

First, Jesus speaks. He speaks to the heart. Do you let him speak into your life? Your heart? Your story? After Peter's attack of envy, "Jesus answered, 'If I want him to remain alive until I return, what is that to you? You must follow me.'" Jesus tells Peter to take his eyes off John and the other disciples and the world and its ways. "Follow me," he says. This from the mouth of the guy who became human and lowly, without looking back or around. This comes from the guy who could rule everything but said to "render to Caesar what is Caesar's."[42] You won't find an envious word from Jesus's mouth. Quite the opposite, actually. Look at his resume:

> *Who, being in the very nature God, did not consider equality with God something to be used to his own advantage; rather, he made himself nothing by taking the very nature of a servant, being made in human likeness. And being found in appearance as a man, he humbled himself by becoming obedient to death—even death on the cross!* (Philippians 2:6–8)

Jesus talked to Peter. He also walked the walk (even on water sometimes). He loved others. He was obedient. He let the downtrodden and the little children come to him. He submitted to his father's will. Peter heard him; Peter watched him. Peter was with Jesus, and that allowed Peter to be with John.

Do you trust God's will for your life? How God blesses and uses those around you—what is that to you? Follow Jesus.

Once we get a glimpse of Jesus at the heart level, we take it to the head level—taking thoughts captive to Christ. The first thing we can functionally do in our lives is identify envy. Use metacognition—think about your thinking.[43] And be honest—quit churching it up, calling it a matter of "stylistic differences" or "personality conflict" or "alternate values set." It is an envy-born hatred you are nurturing toward another parent or a coworker or a neighbor. Identify it. Quote some David: "Search me, O God!"[44] It isn't going to be some complex scavenger hunt à la *National Treasure* either. When we quit playing games, our envy is really quite obvious, and we likely have been worse at hiding it than we think.

Next, confess your envy to God. There is a power in verbalizing it. Yes, he knows. I basically know how my son's day was when he's away at kindergarten. It is kindness that asks how his day went, and it is love that listens to him recount it all back to me. God loves us enough to let us tell our stories back to him. After confessing to

God, confess the envy to another trusted person in your life. We are commanded to do this. It forms accountability and vulnerability, and it is freeing in our lives. Then, if you are really feeling convicted and empowered, confess to the object of your envy. If you do this, make sure it is really a confession. It is easy to do a pretend confession in which you really just accuse and critique the other person. Sin hates to be called out, to be named. In the naming of illnesses, we gain power over them—a plan, maybe even a cure. Sin masquerades as a prince but is actually a pernicious pauper. By the illumination of God's Spirit, shine a light on that dark facade.

Finally, mortify envy. Pray for those you envy. Not that they would suffer and die—you've done enough of that! Pray that they would flourish, have peace, and realize favor in the Lord, with no strings attached. When others around you are blessed, learn to celebrate. Romans 12:15 is a sneaky-powerful verse. It says, "Rejoice with those who rejoice; mourn with those who mourn." This is exactly what love looks like. And if you are a person who rejoices at good news for others and who grieves at the hardships of others, guess what? People will flock to you. Wouldn't it be something if Christians were people's first call when they got a promotion, found out they were pregnant, or came into some money? What if when someone's life washes on the craggy shores of reality with some hardship, you were their first phone call? This verse in Romans is what love functionally looks like. And it is powerfully attractive.

Here's the thing about envy: It reverses this verse. It is the inverse of love. Envy celebrates when lives around it crumble: when the neighbor gets evicted, the boss gets fired, or the celebrity gets canceled. Envy grieves when the neighbor gets a new car, the boss gets a raise, or the celebrity writes a new book.

Envy and love are incompatible actions. No matter how absurd we get culturally, the fact remains that we cannot do opposite things at the same time—I cannot starve while eating or drown while breathing sweet oxygen. I cannot be fully awake and completely asleep. And I cannot foster darkness while nurturing the light. I cannot be ruled by envy and birth forth love.

Meet envy with its antithesis. Be content and practice gratitude: Count your blessings. Be generous: Quit living a get-get-get life and give, give, give of your time, treasure, and talent. Love. Love one another.

One odd thing about love and envy is this: Envy, in some ways, is the greatest evangelism tool ever. Jesus said that people would know his followers by how they love one another. Envy lives in every heart, groping for the next great thing. Materialism and knowledge and power and prestige. More, more, and more. Then it sees a group of people singing together. Washing each other's feet. Bearing one another's burdens. They are rejoicing together over victories; they are grieving together, huddled around hardships. They are not related. They are not the same race or socioeconomic class. They are different ages and possess a variety of abilities. The wanting wanton wanderer of this world sees this image and thinks, with envy, "I want that." With open arms, Love invites that woebegone wanderer, "Come to me, all who are weary and burdened and I will give you rest." Augustine says:

> *Because nothing is more contrary to love than envy, and the mother of envy is pride, the Lord Jesus Christ, the God-man, is both the proof of God's love towards us, and the pattern of humility which befits us men; so that the gross tumor of our sickness might be healed by the antidote of a medicine more potent. Great is the wretchedness of man's pride; but greater is the mercy of God's humility.*[45]

God has withheld nothing good from you. Let us live in the abundance of his lavished love, forsaking the petty scarcity of an ever-comparing world. Come, let us love one another. And as we do, the watching world will know that we are followers of Jesus.

ANGER

*Anybody can become angry—that is easy, but to be angry
with the right person and to the right degree and at the
right time and for the right purpose, and in the right way—
that is not within everybody's power and is not easy.*
—Aristotle

*Be not angry that you cannot make others as you wish them to be, since
you cannot make yourself as you wish to be.*
—Thomas A. Kempis

IMAGINE YOU ARE in your car. No, forget that. We are
imagining, so let's optimize it. Imagine you are in your dream
car. You pull into the parking lot of a busy store, not a care in
the world. You heed the arrows on the pavement and go in the proper
direction—down one lane and then up another. Head on a swivel,
you hunt. Then gloriously: taillights aglow! You see a car preparing

to back up just one row away. You accelerate your dream car, hardly noticing the other vehicles, pedestrians, and shopping carts all about you. You whip the car around and begin driving down the next lane, gliding nearer and nearer to the now-in-motion exiting vehicle. And, by proxy, nearer and nearer to the store. Appropriately, we'll call it Target.

Then you stop. Glare. Another car, facing you and disregarding the directional arrows, is also waiting for the nearly vacated parking spot. You gun your dream engine. Lock eyes with your newfound foe and prepare for battle.

How does it end?

Now, you are reading this in some chair in some office or coffee shop, or perhaps you are in the comfort of your bed. You are relaxed, soothed by the cadence of your own steady heartbeat. So for you, the ending is easy: You gesture at the approaching car, saying, "Go ahead, man! You deserve it." Then you smile and drive on, heroically waiting for another spot to open up. Journey blares over your speakers as you drive on.

The internet tells a truer tale of what happens, though. Don't Google it. Just don't. What happens is hand gestures, limbs flailing. Sometimes, it is vehicles colliding. One person loses a parking spot, and both people lose their minds. Onlookers sometimes join the fray, wrathful Medean lover wounds or yearslong childhood angst fuming to the surface in a parking lot melee.

And speaking of the internet, when you are finished perusing parking lot fracases, frequent any online article ever published and begin reading the comments. Out of the overflow of the heart, the fingers type. People fuming, venting, berating, name-calling—it is everywhere we look.

Anger is a problem.

Now, again, you are sitting, calmly reading a book, so you are also tempted to skip ahead to a sultrier sin, like lust. That is part of sin's power—its ability to convince us so thoroughly of someone else's sins that ours vanish in comparison. Since I don't hit my wife or fight people in traffic, I have no issue with anger. Instead of being able to deal with the actual issue, I am blinded by a greater problem: bad comparison. I am forever minimizing and mitigating my sin by finding someone—anyone—with sins more drastic than my own. I'll even scour the internet for it. Comparison is said to be the thief of joy, but first, it pilfers proper perspective.

The true comparison, when it comes to my sin, should be the one who claimed to be the truth. Jesus is also a fitting contrast to my own anger because we see Jesus's anger on display a few times in Scripture. My favorite of these depictions comes from John 2:

> *When it was almost time for the Jewish Passover, Jesus went up to Jerusalem. In the temple courts he found people selling cattle, sheep and doves, and others sitting at tables exchanging money. So he made a whip out of cords, and drove all from the temple courts, both sheep and cattle; he scattered the coins of the money changers and overturned their tables. To those who sold doves he said, "Get these out of here! Stop turning my Father's house into a market!" His disciples remembered that it is written: "Zeal for your house will consume me"* (vv. 13–17).

Amen! See, anger is cool. I'm fine. That person cuts me off in traffic, I can use a hand gesture to tell him he is number one. When a neighbor offends me, I can fantasize about kicking their door in, doing my best Van Damme impersonation. I wonder if Jesus grunted or had killer karate moves like I do in my visions of vengeance?

Of course, I miss a few things when I compare my anger to Jesus's. First, Jesus is consumed with passion, but it isn't a passion to have his meal prepared just right, or else he is going to attempt to get a fast-food worker fired. No, Jesus's anger is about God—for it is a zeal for God's house. Jesus's anger is righteous. It is looking at human flourishing—or a lack thereof—and doing something about it. I can rain down this same kind of righteous anger, but it also must come with a deluge of discernment because here is the thing about Jesus—he's Jesus. "I and the Father are one," Jesus reminds.[46] I'm not sure I can say the same thing when I am calling someone a moron on social media for saying the *Mission Impossible* franchise is overrated.

When it comes to righteous anger, the Bible is also clear about caution: "In your anger do not sin: Do not let the sun go down while you are still angry, and do not give the devil a foothold" (Ephesians 4:26–27). This sentiment is repeated through the Bible: Proverbs 14, Proverbs 15, Psalm 4, Psalm 37, Psalm 103, James 1, James 4, I Timothy 2, Galatians 5, and so on. Anger, even when concerned with upholding justice, is something we must steward with tremendous carefulness.

That ties in with the second thing I miss when Jesus displays anger in the temple: He makes a whip. I am not great at arts and crafts, but even the Martha Stewarts among us probably take a second at whip-making. And unless Jesus remembered to pack his whip-making Caboodle that day, he probably had to source a few supplies to earn this particular merit badge. We always read about Jesus flipping the script (and the table) in the two temple tantrum scenes and assume he just goes Indiana Jones on the Pharisees. But he doesn't just fly off the handle. It's not him in the corner, losing his religion. Rather, it is him in the corner, fashioning a homemade whip. I have him smiling wryly while he's doing it, bemused at the thought of how many people would use his act of courage to rationalize their own foolishness throughout the ages. I have him humming a gentle song while he worked, the disciples looking on with confusion, "What's that for, Rabbi?" He'd just chuckle the laugh of someone who knows what he is about and what's coming next. Jesus didn't fly off the handle—he made a handle. He thought, he weighed action, and then he proceeded with the proper course. This is not the picture of my anger.

A third thing we can miss in this scene is the point. It is to protect people. To protect people from being barred from God and to protect people from barring people from God. Seldom is my anger—and its action—a propellent for the common good. Most anger seems to take two forms. An explosive, unthinking rage we just wave off as passion or an unrelenting secret simmering we applaud as patience. The first type damages reputation, and the second corrodes trust. Both destroy relationships. So, where Jesus restores relationship, our own anger suppresses or sullies it.

The explosive fallout is easier to spot. Things get broken, people arrested. We go viral for all the wrong reasons. These are the videos that we watch on repeat gleefully—news-making folly, searing signs of the fall.

The secret simmering seething is much sneakier. This is the grudge-holding hatred that lives in snide comments and passive-aggressive gossip. It abandons the chainsaw, rather, cutting off family with a surgical knife. Anne Lamont famously says of this short-sighted unforgiveness that "not forgiving is like drinking rat poison and then waiting for the rat to die."[47] We harbor this sort of wrath for others, for ourselves, and for God.

With anger, though, perhaps it is best not to jump straight to Jesus but again return to the beginning, to that first dysfunctional family that was covered by the decaying leaves of fall. Adam and Eve left Eden and had some children. Two of these were named Cain and Abel. Brothers fight, of course. The scene from *Step Brothers* marches to mind when Brennan defiles Dale's sacred drum set. A donnybrook for the ages ensues, which comes with two important departures from the story of Cain and Abel. First, Brennan does "sin" against his brother—he trespasses and lies. Second, it is fictional and comical. The Cain and Abel story is a real story, both then and now; the tragedy lives within us.

In short, Abel makes a sacrifice to God. Cain makes a sacrifice to God. God is pleased with Abel's heart of sacrifice but not with Cain's. So, while Cain's eventual sin is against his brother, his issue is with God. Here, we get a glimpse of pride: Cain thinks he knows better than God. Cain cannot take responsibility. Cain is proud. And then pride gives way to envy. Rather than meet with God and allow for the heart work to happen, Cain must conjure an enemy, so he finds the person who has what he desires—God's favor. Notice he doesn't just receive God's favor through obedience—again, that would take humility. No, he snatches the wheel and steers for the shortcut without realizing he is driving headlong for a cliff's edge.

Pride turns to envy, and then envy bubbles into anger. *This world has withheld something from me,* the old lies are whispered. The whisper becomes an outward shout of wrath as anger gives way to violence against one another, brother killing brother.

In our own fickle hearts, the same narrative is playing out. It may not end in murder, but it still leaves a mark. C. S. Lewis puts it this way:

> *One man may be so placed that his anger sheds the blood of thousands, and another so placed that however angry he gets he will only be laughed at. But the little mark on the soul may be much the same in both. Each has done something to himself which, unless he repents, will make it harder for him to keep out of the rage next time he is tempted, and will make the rage worse when he does fall into it. Each of them, if he seriously turns to God, can have that twist in the central man straightened out again: each is, in the long run, doomed if he will not. The bigness or smallness of the thing, seen from the outside, is not what really matters.*[48]

In other words, our unchecked anger always leads to death. It brings forth the winds of winter.

It is in this realization then that comes hope and the opportunity for us to return to Jesus. Jesus calls on us to consider how we judge others, alerting us to our tendency to usurp his standard of grace for our own vengeful vendettas. Jesus commands us to love our enemies, which permits us to sober up from the swigs of poison long enough to realize that the villains we've constructed are mostly exaggerated projections—they are flawed people, like us, mostly just looking for a parking spot. Jesus advises us to turn the other cheek, not swing away at every perceived (and often misperceived) slight. He gives us this pristine example of how to walk in a weary world of wrath without lashing out, even as he lashes thoughtfully with the whip of zealous truth.

Jesus's example echoes the wisdom of acknowledging anger but not nurturing it along to wrathful actions: *In your anger, do not sin.* Unlike Cain, we aren't to ruminate and worship the night away at the altar of our anger: *Do not let the sun go down while you are still angry.* Those sleepless nights of wakeful visions of soothing violence should be replaced by healthy acknowledgment, prayer, discussion, and then peaceful sleep.

Emotions are healthy, and the God of the Bible is loaded with them. Made in his image, people feel deeply. But feeling deeply and feeling rightly are not one and the same. Seldom does our decision-making improve when our emotions are ratcheted up. That is why prayer is so valuable a provision—it removes us from the here and now and places us in the transcendent.

Community, too, is another valuable weapon against wrath. Having godly friends who can come alongside us, who can listen nonjudg-mentally, and who can help discern truth from lies falls into the category of the type of love that, indeed, covers (and cancels, I think) a multitude of sins.

Finally, wisdom and maturity are like a nourishing meal that strengthens us for life's temptations. We need to develop both our fight and flight tendencies. How do we fight sinful anger? What friends do we have on call, what journal at the ready, what Scripture in heart, preparing to murder not our brother, but the sin which lays in wait? And how do we fly from evil, fleeing the devil? What am I fueling my body with, and where am I putting myself? What media and music am I devouring—does it invite violence and self-righteous behavior? Does it fuel selfish pride? Where do I look, where do I go, where do I park? Could a change in those answers change the ways and frequency in which I face the allure of anger?

Anger thrives when left unchecked. It morphs into bitterness, then resentment, then isolating unforgiveness. The hint of injustice flares up, and we become secret murderers in our hearts, more masochist than martyr. And then there's Jesus. Hung on a cross of injustice—X marks the spot. Stripped by his own people and mocked, he responded not with scorn. There was no social media tirade, no tantrum, no payback. Out of his mouth, his spirit, came a profound utterance toward them, "Father, forgive them." With that, he paid the debt. When injustice arises against us, we, too, must be willing to begin and end in this same posture, for the debts have been paid. We can fight injustice and take on the wrongs of this world, but not from a selfish, prideful position. But rather a lowly one that is not after glory in battle, for the battle belongs to the LORD. We do not have to rage to prove our value, to earn our worth, to validate our existence, for while we were yet sinners, Christ died for us. We have been adopted by God—accepted, loved, and valued. Living in light of this ultimate debt payment allows us to follow Jesus in the pronouncement of forgiveness; though it might cost us some death, it gains for us and others life abundant.

Now, let's try this again: Imagine you are in your car. No, forget that. We are imagining, so let's optimize it. Imagine you are in your dream car. You pull into the parking lot of a busy store, not a care in the world. You heed the arrows on the pavement and go the proper direction—down one lane and then up another. Head on a swivel, you hunt. Then gloriously: taillights aglow! You see a car preparing to back up just one row away. You accelerate your dream car, hardly noticing the other vehicles, pedestrians, and shopping carts all about you. You whip the car around and begin driving down the next lane, gliding nearer and nearer to the now-in-motion exiting vehicle. And, by proxy, nearer and nearer to the store. Appropriately, we'll call it Target.

Then you stop. Glare. Another car, facing you and disregarding the arrows, is also waiting for the nearly vacated parking spot. You gun your dream engine. Lock eyes with your newfound foe and prepare for battle.

How does it end? Do we resemble more the mob shouting, "Crucify!" or the suffering servant spouting the spring blossom of forgiveness even amid the ravenous death of fall?

When our anger flares up, for me and for you, how does it end?

GREED

The world says: "You have needs—satisfy them. You have as much right as the rich and the mighty. Don't hesitate to satisfy your needs; indeed, expand your needs and demand more." This is the worldly doctrine of today. And they believe that this is freedom. The result for the rich is isolation and suicide, for the poor, envy and murder.
—Fyodor Dostoyevsky

He who is not contented with what he has, would not be contented with what he would like to have.
—Socrates

WHEN IT COMES to the signs of the Fall, it is nice to find a sin I do not struggle with. Greed is one of those. I'm proud of that, which shows I'm not free of pride. And I envy folks who are past pride. Most days, I lust. Really, when it comes to most varieties of sin, I would fit pretty well on the poster. But greed, praise be, just doesn't grip me. Or so I thought.

There are few things I hate more than Starbucks. I delight in being the last American holdout. I will not buy drinks from Starbucks. It isn't some moral position—I'm way too slothful (*boom! another one*) for that. My reasons are purely logical. Most of my life, I haven't been a coffee drinker. But then we started having children, and I was tired all the time and poorer than I had ever been. Enter coffee. You see, there are two beverages you can find almost anywhere in the United States for free: water and coffee. Get work done on your car—there is coffee brewing. Stay in a hotel—there is complimentary coffee in the lobby and sometimes in your room. Head to church, and you can have a hot cup in your praise hand. That verse about God heaping flaming coals on someone's head has, in some charismatic circles, likely taken the form of Folgers. So, with free coffee available everywhere, remind me again why I want to take out a second mortgage to buy a venti cup from Starbucks.

Oh, and that's another thing. What's a venti? What's a skinny-whip cold foam with almond juice frim-fram? I swear it is some kind of Dr. Suess nonsense, listening to people order this stuff.

And then there's the line. Every. Time. There are seventeen thousand cars ahead of you—probably because ordering is like reading Proust aloud. Can't just say, "Small coffee." You'd get judged to the back of the line. I'm getting angry just thinking about it—see, anger! Got that one too.

Now, you are wondering why I am hot and bothered when I said I don't deal with any of this—I don't buy things from Starbucks. Part of the reason for my anger is that I haven't had my coffee today. The line at the car dealership was too long. But the other reason is because when my wife and I go out of town, we stop by Starbucks because she—bless her—likes it. Each visit delays my retirement another year, but loving, godly, romantic husband that I am, I am willing to set aside my own scruples and pull into that ludicrously long line.

On one such occasion, visiting family in Kentucky, we ordered—well, more accurately, she ordered. My wife has to lean across my lap to deliver her coded soliloquy of venti-frim-fram-with-a-zoom nonsense. Then we waited and waited and waited. Finally, it was our turn at the window, and the lady gives me the drink and says, "Well, isn't it your lucky day?"

Doesn't feel like it, I imagined telling her. But I just sat there like a dope, credit card in hand.

"The car in front of you paid it forward. Looks like you got an unexpected blessing."

Did I? Felt like at that moment, with her disparaging gaze searing my face and luring my credit card, that what I actually got was unexpected judgment. Yes, that car had "blessed" us. But also, we had ordered a single simple-ish coffee. I glanced from the woman's waiting, judging face to the rearview mirror. In line behind us was an enormous SUV. I couldn't tell for sure, but I'd say it was a Range Rover full of thirsty venture capitalists. This wasn't a no-strings-attached scenario—it was a full-blown rope squeezing the life out of my stringent budget and moral statutes.

I give to church and to charity. I'll help others along when I learn of a need. Did I need to buy fancy, overpriced beverages for these elite strangers behind me too? I looked at my wife. She was sipping her drink as if it had physically transported her to Italy or something. I looked back at the employee, who was grinning like a cult member that had just been summoned by the All-Mother.

"Bless *you*," I said, and I drove away toward miserly freedom, wondering if maybe I do have a greed problem after all.

Here is a question to consider: What would make your life better? Take a break, sip some cold foam, and actually think on it. If you had one wish for today that would raise your tomorrow, what would it be? Or, if you are having a hard time being honest because this is a faith-based book or something, what would your browser history suggest for you?

Whether you know your answer or not, I bet Amazon does. Amazon: Have you ever heard of it? Well, it used to be a river, but now it is this little company. It began in a garage as a bookseller. Turns out, books don't turn profit—believe me, I know this all too well. What does turn profit? Stuff. All. The. Stuff. This guy in the garage started selling all the stuff and became the third-richest man on the planet—and that, after splitting his assets in a divorce. Turns out being a stuff provider is lucrative.

So, again, what would make your life better?

Scripture has a take on this. My own answer doesn't tend to match the one I find in Luke 12:13–21:

> Someone in the crowd said to him, "Teacher, tell my brother to divide the inheritance with me."
>
> Jesus replied, "Man, who appointed me a judge or an arbiter between you?"
>
> Then he said to them, "Watch out! Be on your guard against all kinds of greed; life does not consist in an abundance of possessions."
>
> And he told them this parable: "The ground of a certain rich man yielded an abundant harvest. He thought to himself, 'What shall I do? I have no place to store my crops.'
>
> "Then he said, 'This is what I'll do. I will tear down my barns and build bigger ones, and there I will store my surplus grain. And I'll say to myself, "You have plenty of grain laid up for many years. Take life easy; eat, drink, and be merry."'

> *"But God said to him, "You fool! This very night your life will be demanded from you. Then who will get what you have prepared for yourself?*
>
> *"This is how it will be with whoever stores up things for themselves but is not rich toward God."*

This passage comes as Jesus is making a speech. It is a good speech. And then it is interrupted by a bit of implied wisdom. That wisdom is this: *Thou shalt not have open Q and A sessions.* When there is a sermon or speech, beware of turning loose questioners. For years, my work required me to set up and run events, and I learned pretty quickly that the idiot always finds the microphone. A speaker will pause, and every cogent person is thinking, *Don't do it. Don't do it. Don't do it!* And then they do it: "Any questions from the audience?"

And as sure as death and taxes, an idiot will find a microphone and ask the expert on race relations—*who is only with us for another eight minutes, mind you*—about her pet cat. The idiot will ask the astute business leader about snow cones. They will ask the author of a book on the seven deadly sins about his chiseled features and obviously robust workout regimen. In one former job, we had an employee who wasn't allowed to ask questions in presentations and meetings of this sort, but the dude just couldn't stop himself, so he ended up banned from attending. He'd have to watch the video version alone later.

Well, here, in this scene from Luke, some ancient version of that banned guy moseys up to the front of the crowd. Jesus pauses for a break or a sip of a latte or to see if anyone has anything to say, and this guy raises his hand and asks a personal finance question. Jesus answers this, "Sir, that has nothing to do with the topic at hand or anyone else present. We are all dumber for having heard your comment."

That is a paraphrase. The exact wording is, "Who appointed me as judge or arbiter between you and your brother?" Which is Jesus's way of saying he's off the clock in that situation.

And then the passage says that Jesus turned to *them*. Jesus is great at this. He would have crushed improv. Here, he turns a loose cannon into a bullet aimed at every heart. And what he says to *all* the people, based on this man's inheritance squabble inquiry is, "Watch out! Be on your guard!"

Brings to mind this one time I heard a bump in the night. It was unceasing and unmistakable to the point where even a coward like me has to check it out. My roommate was out of town, so it was just me at home. From my bedroom window, I could see into our small carport, and there was a dark, hunched figure jiggling the door handle. Either this man was trying to enter my home, or he was a very specific do-gooder handyman who tightens things like door handles in the dead of night for worthy homeowners. Really, it is hard to say which one.

You know what I did? I got back in bed, rolled over, and went to sleep—this breaking-and-entering saga would sort itself out by morning. Or perhaps I left a note instructing the burglar/murderer where valuables were kept and which places on my body were most ticklish.

No! That's not what I did. What I did was start flipping the lights on and yelling stuff like, "We're all awake in here!" and "I have a weapon," and "I'm 250 and chiseled. Ask anyone!" I also called the police. I know deep down I have a latent, special set of skills to handle pretty much any type of physical confrontation, but I figured it is common courtesy to let 911 have their fun.

Turns out the hunched figure was a neighbor at the wrong house at 2:00 a.m. Maybe he was out there sharing the gospel or something. But the police got him home, and I went back to bed. In the darkness of night, I didn't know it was just a confused drunk. Though I make light of it, that was a fearful moment and one that had to be dealt with.

This is what Jesus is saying in this passage: "Watch out! There is a thief at the door to our hearts and minds, violently trying to take life from you." Despite Jesus's warning, what most of us will do is roll over and sleep on. Die on.

Jesus goes on to describe the villain we are to be on guard against. He calls it "all kinds of greed." The word greed can be likened to the word covet—a longing for more of something that someone else has. This is not new from the mouth of God. The tenth commandment is not to covet.

Let's make sure not to miss what is happening in this situation. This silly man in the crowd makes an even sillier comment. Jesus is standing before him—healer, comforter, Savior—and this man is scrolling Amazon, wondering how he can pay for that new Chanel Bible case.

It's like I'm holding a quarter. I look at it, and I see a quarter. But I also see other stuff. I see a desk in the background, and I see the hand of a 250-pound, chiseled man holding that small coin. I see the fingers. But now I move the quarter closer to my face, and I still see some background stuff—things on my desk and such. But I see less of them. The quarter takes up more and more of my vision. Now, I take this quarter, I put it right up to my eye, and it becomes all I can see. The smallest coin can block out the very sun and all its light if held close enough to our faces, our focus.

And that is what is going on with this man in the crowd. He cannot see Jesus, and if he can, it is not as a focal point to reality—it is a mere background prop, a means to a far more important end.

The world's answer to the question of what makes life better is to move the coin closer to our face. Think of the promises that are made every day. Around the holidays, for instance, there are always ads that feature a man surprising his woman with a luxury car only to find out that the woman has also bought the man a luxury car too! They have big bows on the cars and big smiles on their faces, and now they can, in ease and comfort, drive separately to their marriage counseling. The ad depicts us having a better, happier life if we have the better, shinier car, but that car does nothing for our relationships—it brings no healing.

For years, I've dreamed of having a swimming pool at my house. I have a bit of Clark Griswold in me, for sure. Then, one summer, we got a pool membership through my work. We began taking the kids up to the pool most weekends. And I just sat there in a chair. It made me think about when we go to the beach—I just sit there in a chair. I had this realization: I don't like to swim! I don't like being all wet; I loathe being cold; I don't like to swim! Yet I have this fantasy of a better life, one I would spend all my money and my future money on, and then I'd just sit in a chair and hatch a new, shinier fantasy.

We hold these fantasies close to our faces, and they become all we see because that is how the world keeps score. Jesus warns, too, about all kinds of greed. Meaning that we are greedy about family, time, and talent. But, in our modern time of neglected opulence, money tends to be the idol du jour. Greed keeps pushing idols closer and closer to our fantasizing faces. Jesus says, "Watch out! Life does not consist in an abundance of possessions."

Then Jesus tells them a story: "OK, everyone, that was an odd comment about the inheritance. But whatever. Huddle up. We can use this. Once upon a time…" This story is a parable, Jesus's favorite genre. And the story he tells is one of his favorite topics within that genre: money. About a third of Jesus's parables feature money.[49] And that was pre-Amazon. It was in a society that wasn't built on the American dream. Only what if every society is built on some form of the American dream? We act like it is a novel concept to express that getting stuff will make you happy, yet it seems like that sentiment has been in vogue at all times and in all places.

The story Jesus tells begins with a rich guy that we like. He fits our society. He is a farmer who is presumably hardworking and successful.

And then we see how successful—he has too many cars and not enough garage. This guy is awesome—the sort of guy we do biopics about. He's Jay Gatsby without the weird German connection. I want to be this guy.

And with his success, he decides to supersize his life, to make it bigger and better. At the end of all this investing and saving and building, he'd be set for life. He'd rest. He'd sip a margarita poolside, probably sitting in a chair because he doesn't like to be wet or cold.

So that's the old, old story. And it is our story too. A couple things stand out about it.

The first is how often the man uses *I/me/my* language. That's how we do it too: *If I play this right. If I invest wisely. If I take this job at this rate. My portfolio. My savings. My life.* When hardships come, it is all about other people—all their fault. We are quick, in trial, to say, *Why, God!* But when it comes to the good things, the blessings? We cheer ourselves: *Wow, me!* Here is the hard truth that our selfishness will try to squirm away from: It is all God's. It is not my money. It is God's money. It is not my stuff. It is God's stuff. Some of us will avoid this truth by claiming, *But I worked hard for this.* Which is a cute sentiment. It is so perfect that the man in the parable is a farmer. Obviously, that is a very hard job, and he worked hard, so he could make that claim from his chest. But what we could then ask the man is, *Did you make the land? Did you bring the rain? Did you provide the sunlight?*

The same line of questioning topples our haughty, greedy suppositions. Some of us are smart—did you earn that intellect? No. *But I worked hard to learn and cultivate and...* Did you create work ethic? Did you wire your genetics to be hardworking? And let's say you are hardworking completely by your own willful volition. You did this hard work with a working body and with oxygen that was not self-created.

Or let's zoom out a bit. How long could you go without water? Probably a handful of days at most. Likely, three or less. What if it stopped raining worldwide? It just rained nowhere. And that lack of rain lasted, say, three days. That would cause some issues. Probably beyond what we could fathom. What if that happened for three months? What about three years? My bet is it would be game over. All your intellect and hard work would be futile in a world without water.

Don't fool yourself—it's all God's. We are stewards of what God entrusts to us, not sole owners.

Another thing that stands out about this story is the mindset embedded in it. The man says to himself, "You have plenty of grain laid up for many years. Take life easy; eat, drink, and be merry." Do you catch it? The man is equating plenty of stuff with a longer life, with a better life, with life abundant. That's how his logic is playing things out, right? Isn't that our way of thinking too? None of this is really about money. If I were to gift you a duffel bag with a million dollars inside, you'd be pretty pumped. Unless it came with the caveat that you couldn't spend any of it.

We aren't after money. We are after prestige—that's why I wanted a pool. I wanted my neighbors to say, "Wow, Gordon is putting in a pool. What a guy!" We are after power—that's why I wanted a pool. I wanted to be able to invite people over to my pool in order to build and be part of social rings. I'd join in with the other pool owners. I'd give advice to rich people looking to put in pools at their own homes—they'd actually come to me and seek my advice! I want control—that is why I wanted a pool. I could look out on my backyard and be reminded that I am a man who could afford to put a pool in. Hence, I am a man protected. My wealth and comfort can surely buy me out of trouble, help me avoid unemployment, and even aid me in escaping sickness and death. This is an admixture of illusion and delusion.

Some of this is natural and maybe even good. Ecclesiastes says that eternity is placed in the heart of the human. Therefore, a yearning for the transcendent is an inborn tendency.[50] It is why we feel a certain depth of perspective wash over us at funerals. Or, more hopefully, I attended a college football homecoming game that was full of life and vibrancy that felt like it contained the essence of poignant meaning. While this is natural, what is unnatural is to think that a new boat can take me to the sacred shores of transcendence. Or a house. Or a pool. Or savings.

A few months back, I ran some numbers concerning my own retirement prospects. If I am willing to keep my same standard of living and continue my current pace of savings, this calculator reassured me that I'd be able to comfortably retire at the age of 212. It then told me an audacious target number that would allow me to leave work in my sixties. What this machine—and the human mindset behind it—was saying is that if I hit X dollars, I'll be good. At that fantastic threshold, I can rest.

The man in the parable had the same mindset. Rest comes from taking life easy. Then he'd be able to eat and drink—he'd assure his own provision. As a result, he'd be merry—he'd experience the joy he so desperately craved. Those are some big promises, all founded on money and stuff. They are all also counterfeit promises, rip-offs of the same promises Jesus makes: "I will give you rest," says Jesus. He claims to be our provision; we have our joy in the Lord.

Our real problem is that we are all cheapskates when it comes to the soul. It is worthy and weighty, pricey, yet we try to buy it off cheap. Stuff can't bear the value and weight of the soul, though. We need something stronger. We are soul-heavy creatures.

By all external accounts, the man in the story is successful. He is worthy of a best-selling biography. This external accounting reminds me of my son's first soccer game. He was four. And about thirty-seven times in his first game, the ball went into the goal, and no one cheered. A bunch of times, it went into the goal, and the parents acted like cancer had been cured or that they had arrived at a Starbucks with no line. But thirty-seven times, there was nary a sound. The ball control was the same. There was speed. A player delivered a strong shot into the back of the net. Yet the achievement was met with crickets. The reason for this was simple yet profound—the player had scored at the wrong end. He had deposited the ball into the wrong goal.

Success at the wrong end isn't success at all.

We see this play out in the lives of celebrities or big-time politicians. They have duffel bags full of money that they *can* spend. They are powerful and have more prestige than they do cosmetic surgeries. Now find a happy one. The happy ones—the truly contented celebrities—are the outliers. What isn't outlying is the number of the rich and famous that have duffel bags of money and literal duffel bags packed for stints at rehabs. There is an entire niche industry of rehabilitation centers aimed at the rich and famous.[51] This is as sobering as it is unsurprising. Imagine having this clock ticking all the time on your beauty, talent, and charm. Those things have been monetized to buy you transcendence, and yet those things are in a constant state of fading. Your ability to gain transcendence is always decreasing while the cost of it always seems to be increasing. To have everything and still come up short would crush any of us.

Which is why God reacts so harshly to this "successful" man in the parable. "You fool!" says God. You don't see God or Jesus going around calling people fools a lot in the Bible. This epithet is reserved for a man who lives like his stuff is his deliverance and more stuff is his answer. We have neighborhoods, schools, workplaces, and nations of people who do the same. The "you fool" echoes forth.

In ancient cultures, coins were placed over the eyes of the deceased to pay the undertaker to transport the dead to the afterlife/transcendence. We raise the coins of this life closer and closer to our eyes, and eventually, the coins cover the eyes entirely. Forever a coin to the eye has been the sight of death. This man in the parable is focused on what money can afford him, and God says that his soul will be demanded that night. The real question is not how much he has but, rather, if he has been "rich toward God."

Jesus finishes the story and then provides some additional life advice in 12:22–29:

> *Then Jesus said to his disciples: "Therefore I tell you, do not worry about your life, what you will eat; or about your body, what you will wear. For life is more than food, and the body more than clothes. Consider the ravens: They do not sow or reap, they have no storeroom or barn; yet God feeds them. And how much more valuable you are than birds! Who of you by worrying can add a single hour to your life? Since you cannot do this very little thing, why do you worry about the rest? Consider how the wild flowers grow. They do not labor or spin. Yet I tell you, not even Solomon in all his splendor was dressed like one of these. If that is how God clothes the grass of the field, which is here today, and tomorrow is thrown into the fire, how much more will he clothe you—you of little faith! And do not set your heart on what you will eat or drink; do not worry about it.*

Jesus is giving them perspective, and then he invites them to live differently in verses 30 and 31:

> *For the pagan world runs after all such things, and your Father knows you need them. But seek his kingdom, and these things will be given to you as well.*

He is inviting his followers to shift paradigms and break free from golden handcuffs.

I grew up in a river town. Then, in 1993, that river town and every town like it on the banks of the Mississippi were flooded. Once the waters subsided and life was put back in order, a person could get extremely cheap land if they wanted it. Basically, this land was free—a total steal. The reason for the unbelievable deal was that this land was beyond the river wall. It fell outside the protective levies. This land was located where nothing stood between it and the next mighty flood.

If stock A was plummeting and stock B was early Amazon and you knew the future, what would you do? The rational response is to sell off all of A in order to invest in the sure thing of stock B.

What Jesus is telling his disciples—and anyone who will listen—is legal insider trading. He is sharing which land will flood and which land will be forever protected from the raging waters of destruction. Kingdom A is this earth, and the waters are rising; Kingdom B is on an eternal rise. Yet we choose Kingdom A repeatedly. We prove it out in our thought lives. How much thought do we give to our finances, our wish lists, our home improvements, and our raises compared to thoughts concerning our souls? My calculator app gets more play than my Bible app. Even more telling is how often we dwell on our neighbors' homes (paint, pools, and patios) versus our neighbors' souls.

I went from not thinking I had a greed problem to being terrified at the greedy state of my heart and behaviors. And how does Jesus meet my fear—with comfort. "Do not be afraid, little flock," says Jesus (v. 32). I love that phrase, "little flock." He goes on:

> *For your Father has been pleased to give you the kingdom. Sell your possessions and give to the poor. Provide purses for yourselves that will not wear out, a treasure in heaven that will never fail, where no thief comes near and no moth destroys. For where your treasure is, there your heart will be also* (vv. 32–34).

The Father is pleased—get that: *pleased!*—to give you the kingdom. God loves a cheerful giver; God *is* a cheerful giver.

This whole section brings Thomas Edison to mind. He was a man obsessed with light. In his day, darkness meant dark. People who could afford it had candles and firelight Often, it was easier to just go to bed. For those who'd brave the sunless hours, they did so at peril to eyesight and posture as they squinted, mole-like, to read. Edison sought to change all that. He had electricity figured out, along with the vacuum to transport and hold that energy. The hang-up was the filament—without that, there would be no burn of electric light.[52]

Hour after hour, Edison squinted through the darkness, troubleshooting, tinkering, hoping, failing, trying again, failing again. He would sleep only when exhaustion overcame him—and even then, not in bed. He'd snooze for twenty minutes on his worktable and then get back at it. He was a maniac. People in his life became frightened by how joyfully spare he was—he was depriving himself and seemed to be delighted to wither away.

At this point in life, it made no sense to them. Edison was published. He'd invented things already. He had some prestige; he was fine financially. Why? What propelled a man to give up so much?

The answer is that Edison was moved by something greater. He could see the light on the other side. He was content to toil simply, to live meagerly in the present, for the splendid luminosity of the world to come. His gaze was fixed on the world beyond the darkness.

Most of us do the very opposite. We seek lavish, worldly lives of present darkness, thus forsaking the future light. And in that dark choice, the light fades for us. It becomes an unreality.

How do we combat greed when it comes to our material lives? I think a biblical case could be made, first, to make as much money as one joyfully can. *Joyfully* being a keyword in that statement. When we work overtime or all the time, we rob ourselves of joy. But we also must remember that work is part of our reality. We've been gifted talents to put to use, and excellence matters to God. Workers are worth their wages, so we should work well and fairly and earn our living.

Second, we should avoid debt. There is official debt, of course, and it is important to fight it. If you haven't begun that journey yet, now is the time. It is a difficult challenge, but one that is worth it, for freedom is always worth the cost. But there is a second type of debt—the unofficial kind. This is when my desires make me a slave to money. I dream of taking a lavish vacation in the future, so I sacrifice myself and my present for the sake of that future desire. In essence, I am a slave to the future. When the Bible speaks of someone being unable to serve two masters (God and money), it is taking both types of debt into account.[53]

Third, be compassionate and give. Give your money to God. We do this through giving to the church and giving to the poor. For some, we balk at this and say, "Wait, I am poor." We must be careful here, for the poor can be greedy. But the poor can be generous too. The poor widow of Scripture, for instance, has two coins and gives them freely, moving Jesus himself to joy.[54]

Finally, enjoy God's blessings. Make money, give money, and use money. Enjoy it. But don't for a second put your trust in it. The grip by which you hold your stuff is the grip it will have on you.

"This is how it will be with whoever stores up things for themselves but is not rich toward God," says Jesus in conclusion to his parable. Remember how this whole thing started? A man makes a dumb request about his brother sharing the inheritance. In some way, Jesus is reminding him, "Brother, I already have."

> *For you know the grace of our Lord Jesus Christ, that though he was rich, yet for your sake he became poor, so that through his poverty you might become rich.* (2 Corinthians 8:9)

Jesus was rich toward us. He gave his place, his possessions, his prestige, spilling his blood to make us brothers and sisters, co-heirs with him. It is the ultimate pay-it-forward, the most unexpected blessing.

God is rich toward us, and we now have the joy and honor, the great get-to, of taking the coins from our eyes and living our lives in the light of generosity. Let us be on guard against greed, and through generosity, invest our treasure, our hearts, in the unfloodable kingdom of God.

LUST

Greed, envy, sloth, pride and gluttony: these are not vices anymore.
No, these are marketing tools. Lust is our way of life. Envy is
just a nudge towards another sale. Even in our relationships we
consume each other, each of us looking for what we can get out of
the other. Our appetites are often satisfied at the expense of those
around us. In a dog-eat-dog world we lose part of our humanity.
—Jon Foreman

If they substituted the word 'Lust' for 'Love' in the popular songs it
would come nearer the truth.
—Sylvia Plath

Sex is the consolation you have when you can't have love.
—Gabriel García Márquez

I HAVE A JOB. In that job, I meet with people and help plan events. I work for a great company. Then I come home. And if I thought work was cool and busy, it fails to compare to partnering with my wife to raise a gaggle of little humans. On weekends, aside from hanging out and my wife and I trying to keep everyone alive and sneaking in a nap here and there, I sometimes preach at churches who lack discretion, speaking talent, or both. And then comes my third job: I write stuff down and grow extremely rich from my tens of dollars in royalties per year.

Unlike my bank account, with all this swirling around, life can feel pretty full. A person, perhaps sensing this busyness or passive-aggressively complaining about my preaching, once asked me how I come up with the things I say on a stage or write in a book. My answer was that I pray. That is about the only constant because everything else is a moving target. Sometimes, I have ten to fifteen hours to spend on a sermon; sometimes, I have thirty-eight minutes. But God is God, and he is good. Whatever it is he has called you to do, you can be certain that if you show up, he will. Even when time, talent, or sleep are lacking—he is sufficient.

I recall one such breathless week, one of the thirty-eight-minute variety. It was Friday at lunch with a coworker/friend/mentor. I had to preach that Sunday, and I hadn't really had time to put much work into it. Saturday was full of running round town like mad and changing diapers. And then there were my kids to worry about. (Kidding. The diapers belonged to my children. All of them. All the time, it seems.)

You know that dream where you have to take a test but don't know any of the material? Or the one where you can't find the class you are supposed to attend and will flunk out of school? I had those dreams a lot in this particular season of life. All the time, the coach was calling me to go into the game at the exact same time that I realized I had forgotten to put on my shorts under my warm-up pants. That was perpetually the feeling of my life.

Looking back, I am so thankful for the way God works because at that lunch, in that breathless week, my friend Craig brought up a verse that had been bothering him. It was James 4:8, and it reads: "Come near to God and he will come near to you. Wash your hands, you sinners, and purify your hearts, you double-minded." Craig's problem was that the verse is so disjointed. On the one hand, it is so comforting: Come near to God and he'll come near to you. Sign me up! That part gets quoted in about every other sermon and is crocheted on at least half of your grandmother's pillows. But then the verse goes schizophrenic: "Wash your hands, you sinner, and purify your heart, you double-minded." What triggered James? He was totally going to get the teaching pastor gig until he started yelling at kids in the lobby to stop running or they'd burn in hell. What gives, man?

Then it hit me—and it wasn't just the barbecue we were eating. James here is telling us precisely how we draw near to God! We, *sinners*, fight sin! Of course! Sin is what separates us from God in the first (and every) place. He is holy; we are not. Look at the verses that precede and follow James 4:8:

> *Submit yourselves, then, to God. Resist the devil, and he will flee from you* (v. 7).
> *Grieve, mourn, and wail. Change your laughter to mourning and your joy to gloom. Humble yourselves before the Lord, and he will lift you up* (vv. 9–10).

Verse 7 says to "resist the devil." It sets up verse 8. Then, in 9–10, we are told to humble ourselves. Humility is in direct opposition to the chief sin: pride.

I went off. Craig used the word *firehose* to describe my manner. I knew what I wanted to talk about that week. I knew what I wanted to write a book about. It is sin. Fighting sin—conquering it—is how we draw near to God, to love, to hope, to peace. Yet churches and

Christians don't talk about it all that much. And when we do, it is in the abstract—a vague, unspecific manner—or in the past: *We were sinners. Jesus died. Let's sing some songs!*

Craig and I turned to another passage. Right there at lunch. I mean, we were the biggest nerds in the restaurant. Our poor server kept trying to find a break in the Bible rant in order to tend to our drinks. However, not only were we resisting the devil, but we were also driving off a refill.

We flipped our Bibles to Romans 8. Verse 13 says, For if you live according to the flesh, you will die; but if by the Spirit you put to death the misdeeds of the body, you will live. I reminded Craig of how the chapter begins in verse 1: *Therefore, there is now no condemnation for those who are in Christ Jesus.* Paul's point is simple: Refuse sin. Fight. Don't go gently into that dark night. His audience is equally clear: those who are in Christ Jesus—Christians.

Paul talks this way a lot. He uses "flesh" or "old man" or "former man" or "body." So, we come to believe in Jesus, our spirit is renewed, and we are born again. But just like in our natural birth, we still have a body, we still live in the world, and we are still tempted by the devil (sometimes called the "Prince of this world").

By faith, we are illuminated. Enlightened. And, as an enlightened person, we must overcome the body, the flesh, the former person, walking by the Spirit in the light. This illumination (as I'm calling it) tends to follow a pattern. First, we add simple discipline to our faith: We attend church or begin reading our Bible. I was meeting with a new believer once and quoted a few Bible verses at him. After a while, he asked, "Is that the Bible?" When I said that it was, he said, "I have to get me one of those." He did and added the simple discipline of study to his life.

Following discipline, we begin doing actions—there are behaviors we act on. We cease dishonoring God and others with our mouths. We stop getting drunk all the time. We tell the truth.

Then, we start adding things we didn't previously do in our former life, at least not actively. We begin to show kindness and patience. We serve. We give to others with cheerfulness.

Finally, we begin to sift our mindset and attitudes. We get deeper into who we are or, more precisely, why we are the way we are. We determine our whys.

This is the general process of sanctification. And it isn't some three-year plan we age out of. We don't do this till we get confirmed or get some special golden Bible. We do this all the time—over and over and over again. All our days. Sanctification is this great process that we do not, on this earth, graduate from.

Scripture makes this evident in that it is rife with the promises of God. We wouldn't need these promises if the life of faith were a breeze. The struggle is real, so the promises are too. The wisdom of God, too, only matters if, in our enlightened state, we are partners in sanctification. If my holiness were tied robotically to my belief in Jesus, there would be no need for God's Spirit to live in me and guide me. We also wouldn't need one another, would we? The fruit of the Spirit contains self-control—if sanctification weren't real and daily, then why would such a fruit be of value?

A simple way to think about this is that your body is like a phone. Think of one of the old-time phones with the loud ringer. It rings in your life from the day of your birth. It is always ringing with promises of the world—it wants you to act pridefully, to get angry, to lust. And it rings and rings and rings. Then, you become a Christian—you believe in Jesus! And what happens to that phone? Well, it keeps right on a-ringing.

Check out a few Old Testament examples of the phone ringing in the life of a believer:

> *After Saul returned from pursuing the Philistines, he was told, "David is in the Desert of En Gedi." So Saul took*

three thousand able young men from all Israel and set out to look for David and his men near the Crags of Wild Goats.

He came to the sheep pens along the way; a cave was there, and Saul went in to relieve himself. David and his men were far back in the cave. The men said, "This is the day the Lord spoke of when he said to you, 'I will give your enemy into your hands for you to deal with as you wish.'" Then David crept up unnoticed and cut off a corner of Saul's robe.

Afterward, David was conscience-stricken for having cut off a corner of his robe. He said to his men, "The Lord forbid that I should do such a thing to my master, the Lord's anointed, or lay my hand on him; for he is the anointed of the Lord." With these words David sharply rebuked his men and did not allow them to attack Saul. And Saul left the cave and went his way.

Then David went out of the cave and called out to Saul, "My lord the king!" When Saul looked behind him, David bowed down and prostrated himself with his face to the ground. He said to Saul, "Why do you listen when men say, 'David is harming you'? This day you have seen with your own eyes how the Lord delivered you into my hands in the cave. Some urged me to kill you, but I spared you; I said, 'I will not lay my hand on my lord, because he is the Lord's anointed.' See, my father, look at this piece of your robe in my hand! I cut off the corner of your robe but did not kill you. See that there is nothing in my hand to indicate that I am guilty of wrongdoing or rebellion. I have not wronged you, but you are hunting me down to take my life. May the Lord judge between you and me. And may the Lord avenge the wrongs you have done to me, but my hand will not touch you. As the old saying goes, 'From

evildoers come evil deeds,' so my hand will not touch you."
(1 Samuel 24:1–13)

Saul, spurred on by his pride and envy, had hunted David all over the countryside. David is squatting in a cave. Not literally—Saul would be literally doing that shortly. The future king, though, had been made a fugitive. And then the man who had caused all this fear and pressure ambles in unawares to use the bathroom. *Ring-ring-ring.*

The phone rang for David, and pride was on the other end. *You are anointed too. You have carried the nation*, it wished to say. Then anger decided it might as well ring him up. *Here is your chance to take what is yours: vengeance is yours! How dare he use the bathroom in your cave!* The phone rang with anger, and murder was the call waiting. Yet the enlightened man fought. David did not answer those calls. He humbled himself. Then, fittingly, he exited the cave into the light of day—he, too, brought temptation to the light. There, it was seen, known, examined, and declared the monstrous disease that it is.

Now, let's look at the same man with the same Spirit. Yet an altogether different reaction when the phone rings:

> *In the spring, at the time when kings go off to war, David sent Joab out with the king's men and whole Israelite army. They destroyed the Ammonites and besieged Rabbah. But David remained in Jerusalem.*
>
> *One evening David got up from his bed and walked around on the roof of the palace. From the roof he saw a woman bathing. The woman was very beautiful.* (2 Samuel 11:1–2)

Ring-ring-ring. The first time David picks up the phone of temptation is to refuse the call of duty. It was the time when kings go to war. David stayed back. His pride convinced him that he'd done enough at this point in his career, time to rest on his laurels. Then lust dials up David. He sees the woman bathing—nothing wrong with that. Sometimes we see things: big world, lots of people—some of them may not be adequately attired at all times. But David saw that the woman was beautiful. I can walk briskly through a museum. Maybe I am just coming in out of the rain, meeting someone, or looking for a specific work. It takes perusal to adequately assess great art. I have to stop and stare, stand and admire, to call a work of art beautiful. David is lured; then David leers. He can't get off the phone now—the voice keeps whispering.

> *And David sent someone to find out about her. The man said, "She is Bathsheba, the daughter of Eliam and the wife of Uriah the Hittite." Then David sent messengers to get her. She came to him, and he slept with her. (Now she was purifying herself from her monthly uncleanness.) Then she went back home.* (2 Samuel 11:3–4)

David can't hang up on lust. Notice, too, who is with David. He is alone on that roof. He's sending messengers. But where are his friends? Well, those who know him best and can hold him accountable are likely off with the war efforts that he is supposed to be leading. He watches her, learns her, then sends for her and sleeps with her. Darkness wins. David is left alone and in that darkness of his own making. Genesis 4 echoes once more: *Sin is crouching at your door. Rule over it.* David invites lust in and asks if it wants to slip into something a bit more comfortable.

This story is relevant in our day. While greed via consumerism is an American novelty, our other pet sin is lust made manifest through sex. Sex trafficking is pervasive. Our highways are dotted with roadside smut shops. Schools, shows, and art are obsessed with sexuality. Christians have lost their way in the chaos of culture. So, let us begin with what that way is so we can understand how to better ignore the ring of lust.

First, sex is God's idea. Way back in the beginning, we see God charging humans with this: *God blessed them and said to them*, "Be fruitful and increase in number; fill the earth and subdue it. Rule over the fish in the sea and the birds in the sky and over every living creature that moves on the ground" (Genesis 1:28). He tells them to multiply, and he isn't talking about learning their times tables. He's clearly talking about sex and telling them to do a thing that they'd want to do anyway. Why would they want to have sex? For the same reason I want to eat Mexican food—it is good. I like queso. If God were to order me to eat more queso, I'd be pretty pleased to serve that God. We have to eat to stay alive, but don't you also like eating? You likely have a favorite food. In this, we see God's character. He could have just made everything taste like beets—the taste of earth in every bite. Instead, he enriches our lives by flavoring the mundane, adding spice to the mandated. We have to wear clothes to survive, but different textures and colors create fashion. We look upon our world to figure out how to endure, and we are greeted with landscapes and breathtaking vistas, every sunrise an awakened blessing. Procreation didn't have to be pleasurable. It could be like blinking—take it or leave it. Blinking does not make a person moan with delight or purr with pleasure—can you imagine sitting next to that guy at a meeting? I'd change seats. Sex has the capacity to be pleasurable because God is good. He is a just-because kind of God. He is a just-because-love kind of God.

Oftentimes throughout history, the church has struggled with this. Sex has been deemed filthy or pagan. Dangerous. Many a youth group endured scathing lectures on sexual ethics by a repressed youth pastor, and when the sermon ended, they were sent out to be alone and deal with it. So was the young youth pastor, mind you. Complexity and nuance were met with isolation and broad, stern social policing. No wonder why so many Christians have a messed-up sexual ethic. Fortunately, the grace of the cross is bigger than mutated sexual shame.

The idea that sex is shameful was often tragically mated with the idea of marriage. So young people are told that their souls would combust if they felt any kind of passion while growing up, and the notion of sex was heaped with scores of shame. Then the young person was instructed to save all this for marriage. *Wait until you find the person of your dreams that you love the most, and then unleash your heinous desires on them. Oh, and be sure you never really talk about it with them or anyone else either.* This sort of half-truth poison is unhealthy, unhelpful, and unbiblical.

Take Song of Solomon 5:1, for instance: "I have come into my garden, my sister, my bride; I have gathered my myrrh with my spice. I have eaten my honeycomb and my honey; I have drunk my wine and my milk. Eat, friends, and drink; drink your fill of love." This is a guy posthoneymoon who isn't just rolling over in shame. No, he is rejoicing for the good gift of God and the treasure of mate. Sex, like the aforementioned sunrise, has awakened blessing in his life.

We do, however, live in a fallen world. It isn't an everyday honeymoon around here. Which renders sex neutral. It is good per its design. Just as a shovel is good for digging but it isn't great to play catch with, sex is good in marriage and for marriage. But even in marriage we see it manipulated and misused. So how does one ensure sex is leveraged to maximize its intended design in a world gone awry? The answer: relationship.

Sex is intended to be a deep part of a deep relationship. Let's revisit Song of Solomon:

> How beautiful your sandaled feet,
> O prince's daughter!
> Your graceful legs are like jewels,

the work of an artist's hands.
Your navel is a rounded goblet
that never lacks blended wine.
Your waist is a mound of wheat
encircled by lilies.
Your breasts are like two fawns,
like twin fawns of a gazelle.
Your neck is like an ivory tower.
Your eyes are the pools of Heshbon
by the gate of Bath Rabbim.
Your nose is like the tower of Lebanon
looking toward Damascus.
Your head crowns you like Mount Carmel.
Your hair is like royal tapestry;
the king is held captive by its tresses.
How beautiful you are and how pleasing,
my love, with your delights!
Your stature is like that of the palm,
and your breasts like clusters of fruit (7:1–7).

This remains one of my favorite passages in Scripture. It isn't because I am a pervert either. Rather, it is because this one time in Jamaica, a team of us were serving, and we went to visit an infirmary. This place housed older people who didn't have families to care for them. Many of them had physical or mental limitations, and their circumstances were bleak. Yet they had this tremendous joy.

One thing they loved when our team visited was to make us read them passages from the Bible. One guy on our team was going from the women's area of the facility to the men's wing, when a portly old Jamaican woman called him over. He approached the bench she was sitting on and she began shouting at him, "Solomon 7! Solomon 7! Solomon 7!"

He took the hint, took a seat, and turned the Bible to Song of Solomon. A few things happened at once. When he hit the part about *breasts being like a couple fawns*, he realized he was reading Hebrew love poetry to this woman. He also realized that his own wife had come around the corner looking for him. Lastly, he realized that the Jamaican woman, there in the light of the sun, had removed her top and was basking in the sun, enjoying the heat of the day and the words. His cackling wife left him there, and the grinning woman chided him, "Read! Read! Read!" I don't know who was more joyful that afternoon—that dear woman on the bench with her fawns running wild or that man's wife back on the bus recounting the story to us, with her husband blushing the whole way home.

But Solomon wasn't blushing, was he? He was a man in love. He had a healthy, wonderful longing. Much of his sentiment is lost in our culture, but the text is packed with double meaning. He is praising his beloved's physical features, but he is also regaling her dignity, intellect, and spirit too.

In modern romance, love is like a triangle. On one side, we have the biological factors of love—chemicals in us that make us yearn for the physical aspects of love. We will call this "love" because we only have one word for "love." But other languages can more accurately denote love and its many forms. *Eros*, perhaps, is a good distinction for this side of the triangle.

Another side is the emotional. This is where intimacy resides—a depth of relationship. The word for this in the language of the Bible would be *philia*, or friend-love. Where we open up our soul and emotions to another, and where we share vulnerabilities and hidden desires—it is where we are who we really are to another.

The third and final side of this triangle is the cognitive one that thinks: *Hey, I am better with you. You are better with me. We are better together.* This is where commitment lives. We do not commit because the person is perfect, nor do we commit because we are perfect. We

LUST

commit because love wins the day, and then the idea of future love conquers all future days too. This is when we stop just thinking *I love you* and begin thinking *I love you anyway*. We realize that even in the worst-case scenario, we are not going anywhere. The ultimate form of this takes place at a wedding when people stand up before a group of friends and say to one another, "In sickness and in health, till death do we part." I'm not going anywhere.

In sex, we have the consummation of all three sides. That our physical, emotional, and cognitive being unites with the physical, emotional, and cognitive being of another. Absolutely. Completely. It is a soul-level mingling.

What lust does is it removes one or two sides of the triangle. Lust, for instance, tells us that sex is just physical. The world takes the bait and says that sex is not that big of a deal. Think of how this plays out. We divorce sex from God. Then divorce it from the soul. Then divorce it from relationship. Then divorce it from procreation—we've made plenty of advances to remove multiplication from sexual activity. With all of the spiritual components removed, lust is free to corrupt completely. This is why we have a rampant hook-up culture. Just think of how casually that phrase is even used—"hook up." We have apps allowing us easier sexual access. Our shows are bloated with empty sexuality. We are numb to the sexual as, more and more, the sexual has been normalized. Our thirty-second commercials wouldn't be allowed on television in the 1950s. A *USA Today* story found young people agreeing with the sentiment that "sex is less intimidating than a first date."[55] The reason for this is that only one of these things—the first date—requires a level of intimacy. The other is just physical.

This, too, is how pornography works. It is just an "image." There is no personhood, no backstory or future, and, hence, no dignity behind that digital flesh. When this happens, lust cleverly creates a dual slavery: I reduce a person to an image and use them, while they reduce me to my basest desires and use me. At least David had to go to his roof. I contain all the Bathshebas of all the world in my pocket. Fittingly, I access these soul-reducing images and videos through a phone—*ring, ring, ring!* Lust makes sex more and more isolated. It is designed for a pair in absolute union, but it becomes utterly lonely.

And here is the great trap of it all: Lust whispers—our world does—"Oh, don't be such a prude! Get with the times." The paradox is this: The whisper in one ear is that sex is no big deal, while in the other ear, lust shouts that sex is the most important thing on earth. This is why sex is everywhere. A trash can—that is no big deal. We don't think too much one way or the other about a trash can, which is why there aren't books, shows, podcasts, and ad strategies focused on trash cans. If you challenge the sexual ethics of the age or someone's personal sexuality, it is likened to erasing their existence. Not challenging part of them—erasing *all* of them. Why? Because sex is everything. It is totality. It is identity. Even in how we describe ourselves—straight male, gay female, and so on—our sexuality comes first. When we say, in our culture, that someone had a "good time" or that we had "too much fun last night," what we are really saying is that someone got drunk. It is a euphemism that is pretty well understood. And when we say that we are in a "good relationship," what we have come to mean is that we are having good sex—our parts line up well, the friction is good, and the chemicals are doing their thing. Somehow we have removed God, yet we made sex itself transcendent and all-important. We anointed the object. We removed all the fruit from the thing, leaving only the husk, the rind. The substance is gone, and lust, no matter how much we eat, leaves us hungry. C. S. Lewis writes:

> *The monstrosity of sexual intercourse outside marriage is that those who indulge in it are trying to isolate one kind of*

union from all the other kinds of union which were intended
to go along with it.[56]

Lewis goes on to compare this sexual mindset with portraying the act of eating as the chewing up and spitting out of things rather than the whole of the digestive process.

Lust isolates and perverts the act itself. Then it does the very same thing to us. Steve Carell made this joke while presenting an award, "Sound editing is very much like sex. It's usually done alone, late at night, surrounded by electric gadgets."[57] Everyone laughs and laughs at the joke because we've forgotten how to cry at our complicity with a craven culture. The phone rings, and we rush to take the call.

Another trend, when sex is divorced from its Creator and its relational design is to "experiment" with it. Recently, I did a search on Amazon Books for "sex." The advertisements I received in the following days became more and more interesting. What wasn't interesting was what the search revealed. It wasn't interesting because of how predictable it was. Of the hundreds of thousands of results, the first page was littered with books about sex positions, erotic challenges, and ways to enhance all areas of the physical sex act. On and on these listings went. The same sort of promises over and over again. Do you see the trend? Stripped of the emotional and spiritual, sex is reduced to the mere physical. Just one side of the triangle is left. Which isn't a triangle at all, is it? All the offerings, all the gurus, weigh in on logistics and technique. Because that is all that is left.

This is a lie, though, isn't it? Lust lies. We have made sex flippant. It is no big deal. It is just a small bit of fun. We say all these things, yet our lived reality is much, much different. In high school, for instance, I had a herniated disc. It was painful and kept me from sports for weeks, which roughly equated to the end of the world. I had to undergo physical therapy to avoid surgery. I'd do exercises and meet with a trainer sometimes—I had a whole plan in place. Thorough as that plan was, it included zero hours of counseling. My lingering trauma from that herniated disc has never been addressed. I've never been in a group setting and admitted, "Well, it all started with that disc issue in twelfth grade."

Now, what if I had been raped in twelfth grade? Please hear me: I am not trying to make light of that. In fact, I am trying to show the precise opposite: that sex is a big deal. It can be traumatic. And the reason is that it is beyond just physical—it is deep and different. We have moral wounds because we have souls. And these souls are sacred. We cannot treat our souls like they are mere bodies, just as we cannot heal spiritually through physical means. The Bible puts it like this:

> *Do you not know that your bodies are members of Christ himself? Shall I then take the members of Christ and unite them with a prostitute? Never! Do you not know that he who unites himself with a prostitute is one with her in body? For it is said, "The two will become one flesh." But whoever is united with the Lord is one with him in spirit. Flee from sexual immorality. All other sins a person commits are outside the body, but whoever sins sexually, sins against their own body.* (1 Corinthians 6:15–18)

I can't unpack what all of that passage means. But what it is making clear is this notion of different and deeper. The Bible is equating the physical with the moral—uniting body and soul. It is also invoking marriage in the picture, completing the aforementioned triangle concept. God's design for sex isn't changed by our attitude toward it. There is a mystery and seriousness about sex.

Augustine suffered from lust pre-conversion. He was an adherent of a cult that took our cultural position on sex: that it is not a big deal, yet it was worthy of worship. Then, after coming to Christ, and as the phone of Augustine's body continued to ring out temptation, he tried to shine light on lust's schemes in his life:

> It was no iron chain imposed by anyone else that fettered me, but the iron of my own will. The enemy had my power in his willing clutches, and from it, he forged a chain to bind me. The truth is that disordered lust springs from a perverted will; when lust is pandered to, a habit is formed; when a habit is not checked, it hardens into compulsion. These were like interlocking rings forming what I have described as a chain, and my harsh servitude used it to keep me under duress.[58]

Oh yes, lust is a cruel master. The attack is on. The phone is ringing. Total mastery of us is the goal. Lust is never content; it always wants more till we are hollowed out and only dark emptiness remains.

So, what do we do? James says, "Then, after desire has conceived, it gives birth to sin; and sin, when it is full-grown, gives birth to death" (1:15). How do we fight and kill the sin of lust in our lives?

First, we acknowledge we have bodies with struggles. Romans 8 reminds us that God works all things for the good of those who love him. That means he can use our sin and struggle, too. The way God uses those things is that they remind us of our unceasing need for Jesus and unity with others who need Jesus. Twain said, "Be good and you will be lonesome."[59] Fake righteousness, and you will be lonelier still. Lust is a thing, like sex, that we do not talk about. Instead, we isolate. Younger generations do not need more tips on repression.

What they need is to see men and women who put their hands up like Paul and admit, "Yeah, I don't do what I want, and I do what I don't want."[60] The phone rings in our lives—we can admit that. But we can also share the victory of the Lord in our lives. That God has the mercy to forgive, the power to equip, and a love that overcomes.

A friend told me of a marriage panel he went to. On the panel were couples fielding questions, and one couple was in their nineties. A question came from the audience asking them if they'd ever had a rough patch. They admitted to many, but the hardest was the one that had lasted about seven years. Seven years! They struggled and fought and contended for seven years! What a relief to every struggling partnership in that room that day. To know our struggles are not unique is to know that we are not alone because of our struggles. Then to see others who have come through to the other side and seen victory in Jesus means that we can too.

Second, we need to assess our desires if we are to be victorious over lust. "Take every thought captive to Christ" is the Bible's phrasing.[61] When it comes to lust, we must examine our sex ethic as followers of Jesus. And, as followers of Jesus, our sex ethic has to look different than the world's. In all areas, we are either in-step with Jesus or we are in-step with the world. We must, then, ask questions in our own lives, like *What are we agreeing to? What are we conforming to? What are we taking in?* Another Twain-ism says that humans are the only animals that blush because humans are the only ones that need to.[62] Christians, I fear, no longer blush at anything. We have conformed to the pattern of this world. To be free from lust's pervasive poison, we must renew a godly sexual ethic.

Third, we need to deal with stuff. This chapter will end, but your story will not. We need to quit pretending and start fighting. For me, it is a daily battle where I decide and act on if allowing myself to see scantily clad women will help me or harm me in my pursuit of victory? In every decision, in each environment I'm in, am I turning the ringer up or down? The phone will ring, yes, but do I have the wisdom to turn it down? I can also be sure not to go around giving out my number. I can envision my body as being made of wood—dry and brittle. Were this the case, I'm certain I would go to great lengths to avoid fuel and flame.

Avoiding areas of temptation is immensely helpful, as is forming accountability. That Christian men should talk with other men about their journeys; as should women with other women. Married couples should talk about sex—struggles, desires, boundaries, enjoyment. They should also model healthy romance for their children. I want my kids to know that I love their mother; I want them to know that she is the object of my desire, too.

Another way of battling against the guiles of lust is to live wisely with the celibate in our churches. If sex is for marriage, there are a lot of people in our church family living in a wayward sexual culture without a permissible outlet. Think of the unmarried, the divorced, those with declining desires or limitations like age or physical hardship. We must remember that sex is good, but it is not ultimate. Therefore, it is not less-than to be less sexual. We need to strive for relational connection, fullness, and belonging. Together, we love the soul over the body. We bear each other's burdens. We walk in the light.

Last, we keep going. I came across the word *fidelity* the other day. It is a lovely word, and looking it up made it even more fetching. In its definition are words like *faithfulness, allegiance, loyalty.* Also included were accuracy and exactness. It put to mind this faithful exactitude to the way of Jesus, a blessed fidelity. Such a state of unrelenting faithfulness encompasses mind, body, and spirit. We must keep going.

My spiritual home is Michigan. It is where we vacationed for the first thirty years of my life. Long days and nights on the beach, playing volleyball, and the equally back-and-forth rally of growing up all seem to spike during these sacred weeks of summer. It is the first place I gave a sermon. There is nothing like the cool lake breeze on a hot July day—the dunes, the wind, the memories rushing in, wave upon wave. After an eight-year absence, I went back. I took my children to spend a week at my sister's home on Lake Michigan. In my romantic infatuation with the return, I forgot how children are. I remembered how they were when my oldest son, M. J., asked, "Are we there yet?" When he asked this, we were still in our Missouri neighborhood with about ten hours left to drive.

After being asked this question for the ninety-seventh time, I finally said, "We'll stop when we get there. You'll know we are there because we'll stop." This was the absolute answer. It was true. But there were whispers of that very truth all along the way. The air grew cooler as we drove north. Then came a breeze, sweeping across the lakes. We saw rows of blueberries, and we put the windows down to let the air dance across our anticipatory skin. Then we saw water, and it brought a sense of freedom: *We are on vacation. Together and free!*

Back to James 4. It tells us to come near to God, and he'll come near to us. It says we can resist the devil and he will flee from us. In the Old Testament, this fellow named Joseph is sold into slavery and rises in a government official's home. This government official had a government official's wife, likely a beautiful woman. She set her eyes on Joseph, the phone rang for her, and it was lust on the line. She wooed him and entrapped him; she seduced him, echoing the world's lusty claims. And Joseph? With the phone of pleasure ringing in every fiber of his own being, Joseph fled. He ran from her. Ran from lust. Resisted the devil.

In doing so, he ran to Jesus. Ran to holiness. Drew near to God. When we run the opposite way of sin, we run toward the very shores of God. As the people of God, let's drive north together. With grace, with courage, with perseverance, with self-control, and with love, let's notice the signs and feel the breeze cf victory along the way. Let's smell the shore and not go on settling for mudpies in the slum when a holiday at the sea has been offered to us.[63] Let's head north to the lake, our spiritual home, together and free.

GLUTTONY

Swinish gluttony never looks to heaven amidst its gorgeous feast; but with besotted, base ingratitude, cravens and blasphemes his feeder.
—John Milton

Man is what he eats.
—Fyodor Dostoevsky

Things bad begun make strong themselves by ill.
—Shakespeare

ONCE, I WAS preparing a speech, and I got caught up with antelope. I wanted to use the animal as an example, so I began extensively researching them—which translates to: I read two articles. After reading those articles, though, I was kind of depressed because I realized just how little there is to life as an antelope. Roughly, you could whittle it down to about three components.

First, antelope twitch around a lot. An antelope will be sitting there eating breakfast and, every five seconds, will dart its eyes around like it is receiving an electric jolt. It looks here, there, and everywhere, almost all at once. And then, like nothing at all happened, it goes back to eating. Five second pass, rapid twitch and scan, then back to eating. This is constant. I took my boys to the zoo, found the antelope, and witnessed this twitchy paranoia in person. You see, the antelope, after generations of getting eaten by the lion, is always on lion alert. Never, in all of history, have antelopes gathered, as humans would have done, and decided, *You know what? We ran the numbers, and the problem is the lions. We should do something about the lions!* Humans would have painted their faces, shouted freedom, and attacked the lions. Or formed a barrier from the lions. Perhaps we would have gotten on a raft and sailed to lion-less lands or formed a sort of weapon against the lions. Can you imagine a lion-gun in the hooves of the antelope? No way that would end well. Yes, the lions would be in trouble, but, gulp, then what? Well, we really don't have to worry over it because while the lions will always be in the mind of the antelope, the antelope's best long-standing answer is to go on twitching about till grisly death.

A less daunting constant of antelope life is food. Antelope will eat, eat, eat. All the grass—all the time. When the food is gone, they will move on. They eat and twitch, eat and twitch, eat and twitch—no time for books or shows or conversation, not with all this eating and twitching to do.

The third antelope fixture is sex. If antelope are not occupied getting eaten by lions and have plenty to eat, they will get busy, well, yes, getting busy. They want to procreate. This has nothing to do with relationship, mind you. They are not on Antelope Mingle or playing sweet R&B—there is no intimacy going on. It is primal and physical, a survival instinct.

Now compare those realities concerning antelope to this passage:

> Then God said, "Let us make mankind in our image, in our likeness, so that they may rule over the fish in the seas and the birds in the sky, over the livestock and all the wild animals, and over all the creatures that move along the ground." So God created mankind in his own image, in the image of God he created them; male and female he created them. (Genesis 1:26–27)

God doesn't twitch. He doesn't want for food, and he is all about relationship. In this passage, we see the Imago Dei—that humans are not antelope. Rather, humans are made in the image of God. There is a gifted goodness, a freedom, about us. We are special. Called. Unique. Loved. We are not antelope. When we approached lust, we homed in on this ridiculous cultural paradox that says (1) sex is no big deal and merely physical, and (2) sex is ultimate. Somehow, our flesh and world conspire to make sex both lesser and greater simultaneously. To this notion, antelope would say amen if they weren't so busy eating and twitching and mating. They would agree too with the notion of food being the fore-running focus.

This is always what sin is out to do. It seeks to make less of godliness—to besmirch it. Sin wants to break our design, to sully, stretch, and shatter us—like mirrors cracked, we reflect God no more. We live more like the animals we are to rule rather than the royalty we've been called to be. We are divorced from cosmic destiny in our sin, severed from destined difference. We willingly become base beings, less than. We graze the fields of life, hoping for some cheap sex and expensive food along the way, some pleasure, any pleasure. Princely status is traded away for the poverty of a pauper.

Ultimately, this is what gluttony is. It is a shrinking of life. Boiling down transcendence, baking the life from it, and gulping it down without tasting. Then, in our bewildered starvation, we seek more and more of what is hollow, empty. What, again, is that pithy definition of insanity? *Doing the same thing and expecting different results.* Crazed gluttony is thinking that doing more of the same will somehow eventually lead to fulfillment. It is like proposing that a cure for falling down is to fall from greater heights.

When we think of gluttony, we think of food and drink. And the Bible serves a steady spread of these examples. The very first sin involves eating, as Adam and Eve gobble up the poisoned fruit of sin. Then there's Noah, fresh off his flood voyage, getting drunk and naked, and causing family division from his gluttonous ways. Esau would die for some soup, and he ends up killing his own destiny for it. Or take the Israelites who, about ten minutes removed from slavery, want to return to their shackles for the sake of some sandwiches. They looked at God's menu and found it beneath their lofty palate. In the New Testament, the battle of clean and unclean foods forms a racial/ethnic rift that divides the first churches and its leaders.

It is silly to think that so much fuss and division can come from what we eat and drink, but history attests that it does. We can raise any old thing up high enough to bow to. Make anything worth killing for.

What about in your life—what matters? Often, it is best to let life answer. When is the last time you missed church or decided not to help a friend? Personally, I skip church frequently. Sometimes, I almost bail when I'm the one giving the sermon, which would leave the band in a pretty awkward spot. They'd have to play a worship song's chorus like thirty-nine times through to fill the time—wait, I guess that already happens in modern worship songs. Maybe that is why I want to skip church? Singing the lyric, "This is how I fight my battle" *is* my battle. No, thanks—I'm out.

I'll bail on helping others too. I'll convince myself that the friend who is moving probably has more help than he needs or that that particular homeless guy would definitely use my money or kindness to buy heroin or something. So I skip those opportunities too.

How about prayer? Shoot, I'm like three-fourths finished with writing this book and have yet to offer three-fourths of a prayer about it. I skip praying about things in my life pretty much every day.

I am constantly neglecting spiritual, emotional, and relational things. If you are honest, you probably are too.

Now, in that same state of honesty, when was the last time you skipped lunch? People leave churches for going long—probably from doing that chorus for the thirty-ninth time—and upsetting their sacred lunch plans. And don't get me started on dinner. Breakfast? That's the most important meal of the day, right!? Jesus says, "I am the bread of life," and between mouthfuls we mumble back, "Wanna bet?"

In the book of John, Jesus heals a bunch of people. In that time in his ministry, this was like a Tuesday for him, NBD. But on this one particular day, Jesus takes it up a notch. After he heals people, more and more people keep following him. The problem is, there are no restaurants nearby. The antelope are grazing on a dirt patch—not an Applebee's in sight. So Jesus feeds five thousand men (and a bunch more women and children too). He turns a Lunchable into a veritable buffet, complete with leftovers. And here is the response of the people: "After the people saw the sign Jesus performed, they began to say, 'Surely this is the Prophet who is to come into the world.' Jesus, knowing that they intended to come and make him king by force, withdrew again to a mountain by himself" (John 6:14–15).

They saw Jesus do something remarkable, and so they wanted to make him king. Do you see what is missing here? Do you see what is elevated? It is not Jesus that is lifted on high in this scene—it is lunch. They have physical needs. They see a man who can meet their physical needs. OK, where do we sign the paperwork—let's anoint this thing!

A few verses later, we get their reaction to Jesus's departure: "Once the crowd realized that neither Jesus nor his disciples were there, they got into boats and went to Capernaum in search of Jesus" (John 6:24). They wake up and want breakfast, but the Messiah chef is gone. The Burger King of kings has left the building. Now, in between their hunt and his departure, a thing happens. It is a minor thing. It is penciled into Jesus's calendar: *morning – heal the people; afternoon – feed a decent-sized town of people; evening – take a break and walk on some water.* That's right: He walks on water. My kid one year wanted this remote control car that claimed to cruise on water. He asked for it day and night for months. The day of his birthday came, and he just got an empty box instead and the offer to say the "Sinner's Prayer." I figured I could give him a car that would sink or a man who wouldn't. *Jesus, bro, free gift.* I saved a ton of money that birthday. Also, got a divorce thrown in.

I'm kidding. I got him the car. And it did sink. And for many Christians, their hearts sink a bit when scenes like this pop up in the Bible. Jesus saying smart stuff is cool—we like that. The golden rule stuff, that's an easy sell for us with unbelievers. But then we come across these sorts of miracles, and we stumble. We are embarrassed. No one can walk on water. Well, the Christian and the skeptic agree on that. And that should be comforting. The difference of belief between the Christian and the skeptic is merely one person. Jesus walking on water doesn't mean that everything is possible for everyone all the time, always. It doesn't mean I am going to jaunt down the Hudson anytime soon. It means that Jesus walked on water. That he is the singular person in history who could do this sort of thing—or empower others to do similarly miraculous things. The skeptic and the Christian do not have to believe in every single impossible idea. Just in one impossibly, possible one—in Jesus.

So, Jesus heals, then feeds, then walks on water. A search party is sent looking for him, and when they find him, here is what plays out:

> *When they found him on the other side of the lake, they asked him, "Rabbi, when did you get here?" Jesus answered, "Very truly I tell you, you are looking for me, not because you saw the signs I performed but because you ate the loaves and had your fill. Do not work for food that spoils, but for food that endures to eternal life, which the Son of Man will give you. For on him God the father has placed his seal of approval." Then they asked him, "What must we do to do the works God requires?" Jesus answered, "The work of God is this: to believe in the one he has sent." (John 6:25–29)*

The people here are channeling Oliver Twist, "Please, sir, may I have some more, please?"[64] This story puts me back to the time that I visited a buffet in London back in college. I had very little money and hadn't eaten much in my travels, so finding a buffet at which to spend ten of my last pounds (and gain a few bodily pounds back) was a sublime discovery. The catch was this buffet was designed to be one trip. You could pay for the standard one trip, or almost double your payment to upgrade to all-you-can-eat. Now, those Brits may be smart and talk pretty fancy, but America is the land of skyscrapers, and I paid the one-trip fare and made a skyscraper of my own there on my plate. This thing was a towering mess of meat and salad and cheese and dessert. "Jolly good, jolly good," I muttered mockingly at my hosts, proud of my frugal savvy. Only the fix was in! When I got to the end of the line, they had an employee working a scale. He measured each plate, and there was an upcharge based on weight, and my tab was as lofty as the tower of food on my plate. I left with a full, sick belly and empty, sicker pocketbook.

With Jesus, these followers are doing just that—they are after more of the same. They want to keep piling their plates higher and higher without realizing that Jesus is offering an entirely different meal altogether. They are stuck like Esau, desperate for some soup. And he is there, like that buffet worker, weighing their hearts.

And then comes verse 30. It is frustrating: "So they asked him, 'What sign then will you give that we may see it and believe you? What will you do?'" Do we need to recap the last thirty-six hours? Jesus had just done some Aes Sedai–level healing. Then he'd made the valley into the original home of throwed rolls. To cap it off, he literally moonwalks across the water that night. And they have the temerity to ask for a sign!

Audacious as it is, it is precisely what some of us are doing right now. We think things like, *If I could only see Jesus do these things. If I could only witness a miracle.* Billions of people have believed the nutty story of Jesus. The Bible is thousands of years old, yet people still read it. It is jammed into hotel room drawers. It is a hard read, too. And it is offensive—it calls everyone a sinner! Yet people keep seeking it, reading it, being moved by it. Then there is every sunset, every birth. Each breath. The stars. Great art. The roar of an energized crowd, the feel of a first kiss. Come on. If you haven't seen enough signs by now, you will never be satisfied. Likely because it isn't really signs you are after in the first place. That is just the excuse your pride is comfortable hiding behind.

Now, I do want to give these ancient folks a little grace. I'm an American, and as such, I know where my next meal is coming from.

Everyone reading this sentence will eat this week. Even some of us who are quite poor and have hard lives have a way to get a meal. These people, however, had no food storage or access to refrigerators. They didn't have drive-through windows on every corner preparing meals to order. In those days, save for the extremely wealthy, it was hard to eat. By the sweat of the brow, folks would get dinner. And now, suddenly, they found this living, breathing vending machine rabbi. This would remove worry from their lives. In our modern times, this would be like Jesus giving out $10,000 to a bunch of people. Recipients of this gift would rejoice, count their blessings (and their money), and then, in about three days, go find Jesus to see if another 10K was coming. We crave material things. The people following Jesus had a different craving, yet pursued Jesus the same way we do: not for being the Almighty but for potentially providing an almighty payout.

They go on in this frame of mind in verses 31–33:

> "Our ancestors ate the manna in the wilderness; as it is written: 'He gave them bread from heaven to eat.'" Jesus said to them, "Very truly I tell you, it is not Moses who has given you bread from heaven, but it is my Father who gives you the true bread from heaven. For the bread of God is the bread that comes down from heaven and gives life to the world."

The people here are thinking back to Moses and his MRE provision. Jesus redirects them, though. The food back then and the food today, he reminds them, is from God. It is all God's. Food and drink are God's ideas. Crops and animals, weather patterns and sickness, all the things pertaining to our daily bread falls under God on the org chart of this world. Every bite, then, is a sweet provision from a kind

SIGNS OF THE FALL

God. Now add flavors to the mix. Come on! It is like gifting someone a house, and then they find out it is fully furnished. It is finding
chilled water bottles in the cupholders of the car you are borrowing
from a friend. Everything is from God.

Gluttony is, at the primary level, forgetting that. It plays out in
various ways. Thomas Aquinas had a breakdown of gluttony because
Thomas Aquinas didn't have social media. That is what people did
before the internet—they'd do systematic breakdowns of things like
gluttony.[65] This is also why Thomas Aquinas probably didn't get invited
to many dinner parties.

First on his list of gluttony is the consuming of food and drink
"hastily." When we eat or drink without regarding the provision of
God, we are engaging in gluttony, according to Aquinas. The same
week I learned of Aquinas's list, I visited Arby's. I was in a hurry because
I had to write a sermon on gluttony, but David, the drive-through guy,
didn't seem to care. "Would you like to add our new mac n' cheese?"
he asked. After I declined, he responded, "How about a drink to go
with that?" I had my own drink, so again, I re*beef*ed his advances.
"Would you like two cookies for three dollars?" Of course, I wanted
two cookies, but I was mad at David for pushing it. This irritableness
showed as I snatched my roast beef, cheese sticks, and cookies from
smirking David at the window. Then I proceeded to wolf it all down
as I hurtled my car through traffic—I only had about a thirty-minute
window to work on my talk. I wrote a sermon on gluttony with a
marinara-stained face.

Aquinas notes "too expensively" as his second gluttony indicator.
"Follow the money" is a popular investigative maxim, and it is true of
spiritual things too. Where we place value and spend money reveals
what we worship—where our treasure is. If you can only dine on the
fanciest fare, then it is likely you are ensnared by gluttony.

Third on his list is quantity. Aquinas focuses here on the type of
gluttony most of us think of: when someone eats or drinks more of

something than they should. I would add that eating or drinking less than one should might also be a form of gluttony. Both ends of the spectrum reveal a trust in one's self. Our diet is a thing that we control, thereby building that trust more and more. I trust myself so much that I can have one more drink or cookie. Or one less. And soon, we fall in the trapdoor and lose control. One more becomes one more every time. We wither away or gain a sizable waist. Our bodies become our gods, and our meals our master.

Finally, Aquinas claims that those who eat "daintily" may be engaging in gluttony. What he is getting at with this one is entitlement. When every meal becomes a life-or-death decision, when we put food and drink ahead of people. When we are demanding or petulant over a pickle. Think of a time when you asked for a burger without pickles only to find the disgusting green pads littered all over said sandwich. Pickles are the worst! (And if you are a person without taste and disagree, then substitute whatever it is you want held off your burger—maybe common sense?) You pull away from the drive-through, unwrap your lunch, and see the horrendous mistake seeping into the bread and meat. Don't you just lose it? You want to send an email. You want to storm in and rub that burger in some dolt's face. You want to demand accountability from the minimum-wage employee who is ruining your life. There needs to be accountability! Someone should be fired! Well, that, folks, is gluttony.

I recall going on a service trip to an impoverished village with a team of Americans. We were building small houses for villagers alongside a team of locals who were the ones *actually* building small houses for villagers. During a break, as we awaited a supply of cement to be delivered, the Americans lounged at the worksite and began talking about food. We were naming our favorite restaurants, belittling the preferred places of our friends, listing off desserts, comparing Cobb salads, and ranking the best steaks in town. My mouth was watering after a handful of days of sparse accommodations. Then I noticed the work team of locals. They had been listening to our discourse—these slender men who lived on one to two meager meals of rice and beans a day. Gluttony can be spotted when food and drink make us unloving, unaware, and ignorant of other human beings.

It is just another of our disordered desires. Food, like so many things, is neutral in a fallen world. It can be a good thing—it can generate gratitude and create community. One of the main causes of nostalgia is smell.[66] We breathe in the smell of homemade cookies, and we are reminded of Grandma's cookies; we are moved to a world we can never have again. Never, unless... unless everything can and will be redeemed, remade. Even the cookies. Food can also be good in that it is yet another way we reflect God as image bearers. When we apply our artful, creative sensibilities to cuisine we are mirroring a God who makes things good and very good.

The question then is, do we consume food and drink, or does it consume us? Revisiting *The Lion, the Witch, and the Wardrobe*, we witness Edmund becoming a traitor to his family and abandoning goodness.[67] Part of the allure of the series of books is to see Edmund's transformation from darkness to light. But before the light shines in his life, darkness is deeply established, and food is the method it uses to bind Edmund and blind him to the light. "While he was eating," the narrator describes, "the Queen kept asking him questions. At first Edmund tried to remember that it is rude to speak with one's mouth full, but soon he forgot about this and thought only of trying to shovel down as much Turkish Delight as he could, and the more he ate the more he wanted." The Queen mentioned in this scene is wretched. Everyone can see it. Everyone but Edmund. He cannot see anything but the sweet treat before him. Later in the book, we find Edmund ever more ravenous for this bewitched Turkish delight, only it can never quite appease him—he always craves more and more and more. He is addicted; his desire is disordered.

Similarly, food and drink can turn us into beasts. At a parade recently, I was cheering my boys to grab more and more candy. This went on for hours, and I noticed other parents doing the same. Children were scrabbling and scraping for more and more of what they already had and what they didn't really need in the first place, with the watching world applauding their efforts. I had a vision of antelope flash before my eyes.

My wife and I watch a television show called *Survivor*. We never miss a season. In season 45, the show highlighted a hapless contestant named Jake. Jake had a problem on the show—he kept passing out. He'd be doing regular camp chores and just crumple. This seemed to be a fairly ineffective strategy on a show whose tagline is *Outwit. Outplay. Outlast.* After one of these blackouts, Jake became increasingly emotional. He could hardly get the words out to tell his story, stopping several times to sob. Turns out, Jake had been incredibly unhealthy. He had become more and more addicted to food and engaged in destructive binge eating for many years. To get on the show, he battled his compulsion and lost well over a hundred pounds. The impetus for his change was a family event. He drove to his parents' house, and before going in, he was in the car, hiding and eating—wolfing down every last bite he could. His mother approached the car without his knowledge, and he was found out. There he was, caught and covered in sin and shame. He rolled down the window, and his life changed. His mother said, "Jake, you don't have to hide. Come inside. We love you."

That should be the slogan of every church: *You don't have to hide! Come inside. We love you.* Those are the words of love. Those are the words of Jesus. "Then Jesus declared, 'I am the bread of life. Whoever comes to me will never go hungry, and whoever believes in me will never be thirsty'" (John 6:35). Jesus sees us on an animalistic path. He catches us in our sin, hiding away our shame. And then he says, "Come inside, I've got something better for you!" The pagans in Scripture are depicted as saying, "Eat, drink, and be merry—tomorrow we die." But Jesus offers another way. He offers life abundant in place of death. He offers freedom.

Picture a curmudgeon homeowner with a bee issue. Each day, he tries to get the bees, but the bees do what bees do: They fly away from his snares and wrath. Bees, after all, were made to fly. Then he comes up with a scheme, "Let them aid me in their own destruction." So, on day one, he lays out honey, and the bees come carefully and eat it. On day two, he sets out more honey, and the bees, again carefully, come and consume it. On and on, more and more honey each day. Within a week, the bees are swimming in it. And that is when he approaches with a flyswatter in hand. The bees attempt to fly away, as they had always done at his devious approach, but they can no longer fly. They are fat and sticky in honey, their wings unmoving. The homeowner dispatches the bees one by one. John 6:66 is a tragic verse that tells the same story: "From this time many of his disciples turned back and no longer followed Jesus."

Gluttony is a constant threat. It is deadly alive in many of our lives right now, weighing us down and perilously forbidding us from spiritual flight. But most of us read chapters like this one and feel really good. We attend church and get all convicted about the different sins that buzz around our lives. And then we leave—the books, the services, the retreats—sad. Because, though we can see it all at the head level, at the heart level, we don't really want to change. But God's Spirit is shining the light—He is opening the eyes of our hearts. We are being activated and empowered to fight and overcome darkness.

To follow that light when it comes to gluttony, we need to identify it in our lives. We must recognize the sneaky grip sin has on us. Take alcoholics, for instance. None of them are alcoholics. They rationalize, spin, curse, blame. Between secret swigs, they deny, deny, and deny. None of them are alcoholics, and none of them can get help until they are. But what a delight it is when that light breaks through. At the eighteenth meeting, they admit their plight—they name their abuser. They don't even have to say a word. There is a tearful readiness that has taken root. Realizing they are whipped, they take up the fight. It is a lovely thing to witness. It is Edmund going from sniveling turncoat to loyal king. It is transformation It is that brilliant realization that today is the day that any of us in Christ can leave freer, fighting and overcoming.

When it comes to food and drink in your life, are you secretive? Overly selective? Zealously committed? Are you controlled? If so, you just need a different focus. As the old song says, "The things of earth will grow strangely dim"—that is what we are after.

An old warden was once lamenting the waste of a death row inmate's last meal. It wasn't that he was inhumane in his scruples. The warden's complaint was that the food for a final meal routinely went untouched, for a man mere hours from meeting his maker had more pressing matters on his mind. The things of earth were dim, indeed. For the believer, we must be about kingdom business. Food and drink are fine and good, but we serve a better king. There are more pressing matters.

If you want to test the gluttonous areas of your life, take up the age-old spiritual discipline of fasting. What fasting aims to do is to set your spirit-infused will against anything. I can fast from entertainment, even though the world seems to clamor that I need to watch every single new show on earth to be relevant. I can fast from watching sports—I had a friend who did this. He played Division I football and was a glutton for his alma mater. His weekends lived and died on his team's performance. And then, one season, he gave it up. He didn't want it to have a hold on his heart, so he gave up his season tickets, stopped watching the games, and just rested on the Lord. He missed a great season, but he gained a trophy far surpassing any earthly championship. We can give up food and drink or certain types of food or drink. We can give up—and this one might cause you to pause and possibly judge me—religion. We are the first people in history who can listen to seventy-nine sermons a week. We can spend hours in the Bible every day. Yet, for all of our religious toil, many of us do not seek Jesus. Know how I know? Because we don't love our neighbors. You see, loving one's neighbor was a pretty big deal to Jesus, so when we avoid our neighbor so we can do one more Bible study, we are stepping over the wounded of our world rather than taking up our Lord's words and being like the Good Samaritan.

Daily, we should pause and say, "Search me, oh, God." But we don't say that—we are scared of repercussions, and rightly so. There is one big repercussion in showing God our sins. It's this: A God who sees that secret sin will answer, "Well, I'll just have to go ahead and die for that one too. Now, let's get back to it, my precious Image Bearer." The repercussion has already happened—Jesus faced it on the cross. Now, in power, he says, "Come in. I love you."

Another step we can take in battling gluttony is to renew our purpose. In 1 Samuel, there are some wicked priests. They start small, taking shortcuts in the sacrificial system. They begin taking extra meat for themselves. Eventually, they are using their standing to sleep around. As a result of their wickedness, death comes for them. One of these priests died while his wife was pregnant. The woman has the child and names him "Ichabod." This name translates to the word "inglorious."

The glory of the Lord departs when we are about perks. Goodies. Extras. We are made by God, loved by God, and our chief end is to glorify God and enjoy him (and his gifts). If that is our chief end, why are we hellbent on shortcuts leading the other direction? Why are we settling for snacks when he offers a bountiful feast?

One can find this in our modern churches. We clamor for the best music teams, the most eloquent pastor, the most splendid facilities. We use our church for social networking. In these things is the power. With this view, we exchange living for dying.

Life is to be lived on purpose, in purpose, and with purpose. Antelope eat, have sex, and then they eventually get eaten. They invent nothing. They share nothing. They birth no joy, no love, no legacy. We need to renew the purpose for which we were made. Who are you in Christ? Who were you made for? Answer honestly and then quit settling for earth's best impression of God's kingdom.

In short, we must choose freedom.

Antelope have a cousin called the African impala. Cars have been named after this impressive breed. The impala is wildly athletic. It can jump something like twelve feet high, which makes farming impala a nightmare. To keep impalas contained, a farmer needs a lot of land for them to graze on, and then enough fence to cover all of that land. And the fencing has to be at least twelve feet high. I'd make mine thirteen feet in case I happen to have the Michael Jordan of impalas.

These needs made impala farming far too costly. Farms were dying out left and right. All but one. One farm was crushing it. While everyone else was going under, they were rising high. A visit to the farm told the unexpected tale—it was all about the fences. This farmer was using fences that were only four feet tall! Did he know nothing of impalas? A single effortless bound and his impala would be free. Only they did not bound. They did not flee. They stayed right where they were—completely captive. And here was the key: the fences were opaque. Turns out, African impalas will not jump if they cannot see the other side.

It is time to jump. The other side awaits. We can be free of gluttony, but we must act. Write down what God is revealing about your heart. Tell someone about it. Don't be like the squirrel I saw the other day. I was driving to work, and this squirrel darted out into the road. Then the squirrel changed directions about ninety-seven times as my vehicle got closer and closer to crushing it.

Ever see a squirrel cross the road without a car coming? It is totally normal—the squirrel runs across the road. That's it. The whole story. You see, the squirrel's problem is predominantly my approaching vehicle! Remove my vehicle, and the little squirrel heart beats at a normal rate—there are no strong emotions.

Humans are like this. We do not make wise decisions when emotions are high. Think about the last time you made a big mistake or about some relational fallout that occurred in your life. It is likely that the scenarios you come up with have two things in common: (1) They probably include intense emotions—a proverbial car is headed in your direction; and (2) someone probably saw it coming. The squirrel in the road needs a squirrel on the side of the road shouting, "Straight on, Chip! Go straight!"

And so do you. Wisdom is oftentimes just the product of outsourced thinking. You seek many counselors with many vantages, and you have a better understanding of which path to take and which to avoid. You also lower the emotions.

Know what a single glutton is? A single glutton. Know what two aware gluttons produce? Less gluttony. There is a higher likelihood that one in a pair of gluttons is clear-headed enough to say, "You know what, Dale? You've had enough. Let's call it a night."

By following that same logic, what if you have four aware gluttons? Seven? A few hundred in a family called a church? This is why the Bible tells us to bear one another's burdens. With enough love and care, they are no longer so burdensome.

You think about Jesus claiming to be the bread of life, and then you think about bread. Bread is grain that is beaten into flour. Then the bread is baked at great heat. Next, it is broken into pieces. And that is how Jesus proves to be the bread of life for you—he is beaten, placed in a crucible of heat and hatred, and broken. And just as bread, when consumed, nourishes us, Jesus feeds us life. He sets all things in their place, allowing us to enjoy God, bask in his gifts, and leap into sweet freedom together.

SLOTH

Thou seest how sloth wastes the sluggish body,
as water is corrupted unless it moves.
—Ovid

Sad will be the day for every man when he becomes absolutely con-
tented with the life he is living, with the thoughts that he is thinking,
with the deeds that he is doing, when there is not forever beating at
the doors of his soul some great desire to do something larger, which he
knows that he was meant and made to do.
—Phillips Brooks

I HATE RAKING THE leaves. It is prehistoric, tedious, and, most times, proves to be pointless. Bent frame, borne back ceaselessly and all that, I rake and I rake and I rake. Then, afterward, I look at the pale green grass contentedly and begin cleaning up. Snatching up the last rake, I head for the garage when a single leaf dances down from above. Then another. Then another. Within hours, it is like I was never out there. It seems futile, so I take up the remote control rather than taking up the fight.

That is a picture of sloth. We can spend all the time we want thinking about sin, game planning some future time to rake up the lawns of our lives, yet our intentions are rendered pointless if sloth is present. Sloth invites all the other sins. It makes us easy prey. It weakens us. Sloth turns us from the hunters to the hunted and then from moving targets to sitting ducks. We lie in wait for our destruction.

Misunderstanding is a key to sloth's danger. When it comes to sloth, we think of the fuzzy animal that sleeps a lot. It is endearing. As a four-year-old, my son was a collector of stuffed animal sloths—it was his favorite animal. Or we think of a person who doesn't rake his or her lawn. We think of someone who is lazy at their work—a flabby body with flabbier habits. Physical laziness can certainly be a byproduct of sloth. The Bible, especially Proverbs and a few parables, deal with this sort of laziness. But this type of sloth is often a branch; we need to be a people who go for the roots.

Ever dislocate something? I've had this happen with my finger. It is an odd and painful experience—your finger being out of alignment. In part, it is not where it belongs. Therefore, it cannot function per its design. Left like this, it will mostly bear the appearance of a finger, but in function and effect, it is no longer a finger as a finger ought to be.

Physically, dislocation is bad. Emotionally, it is far worse. Take twins separated at birth, for instance. In Bogota once, there were two sets of twins: twins A and B and twins C and D.[68] Well, C and B got switched at birth somehow. When a series of events led both sets of twins back to each other as adults, it was emotionally straining and difficult at first—there was an acclimation to this unforeseen reality. These double twins survived and even thrived, but there are worse situations. Ones, sans reunion, that end in mental health crises and even death. When these circumstances occur, the parties involved just sort of feel it—they feel like something is missing. A dislocated finger is bad; a dislocated heart worse.

With that in mind, we turn to the eight deadly sins. No, that is not a typo. We know the seven deadly sins, yet when theologians were trying to study sin and come up with a list of cardinal/capital sins, there were originally eight on the list.[69] At some point, they had a merger in which two sins became one. So, in essence, one deadly sin is comprised of two parts—it is a terrible two-for-one. And that sin is sloth.

The two parts that became sloth describe a dislocation. It is a physical and emotional dislocation. It creates a dislocation of the soul. The first part of sloth—twin A, if you will—is *acedia*. This archaic word means "apathy, feeling lukewarm or numb." Its other half—twin B—is *tristitia*, which means "sadness." But this isn't the mourning one feels when they miss a green light or can't get into the restaurant they are craving. It is much deeper, a sort of bone-deep sensation. It is the empty, littered stadium three hours after the big game when all the cheering has stopped, the fans have departed, and only the trash swirling in the dark, winter chill remains. We begin not caring a little until, eventually, we don't care a lot, leaving us with an unrelenting weariness of soul.

Here is how David Brooks describes it: "Acedia is the quieting of passion. It is a lack of care. It is like living a life that doesn't arouse your strong passions and therefore instills a sluggishness of soul… like an oven set on warm."[70] An oven that cannot bake anything is no oven at all, mind you. And when he speaks of sluggishness of soul—well, that is sloth. He goes on, "The person living in acedia may have a job and a family, but he is not entirely grabbed by his own life. His heart is over there, but his life is over there." In this state, if your life popped onto your television screen, you'd yawn and turn on *Seinfeld* reruns—a show about nothing is better than a life about less. The soul is dislocated. It cannot function per its design. We feel this like we can sense a storm coming on.

As for the sadness part of sloth? We can turn to someone we care way more about than David Brooks. Shoot, most in our world favor this person over Jesus. In Taylor Swift's lyrics from "Evermore," she hauntingly captures these feelings. Swift describes a deep, peculiar pain that isn't traced to some glaring trauma or physical injury. Some wintry deadness has seeped into her existence, and the result is a feeling of unsettled isolation, along with an almost forgotten sense of what it was to feel purpose. A gray fog has rolled in, only it doesn't, on Sandburgian little cat feet, move on. It settles in—a forever grayness.

The song comes around with a pick-me-up turn, but preturn, it masterfully captures a deep sadness. Worldly concerns and disappointments have become ultimate. Circumstances have been catastrophized to the point of seeming hopelessness. Letters are sent to the fire, an oven on warm. Ultimately, despair looms. Beyond mere romance, those lyrics describe our spiritual state. Our spiritual light has dimmed enough to progressively darken us—evermore. We have become spiritual Eeyores, stuck in a land of friends and adventures and honey, yet blinded by the trees. Lost among the pines and willows of apathy and sadness. Dorothy Sayers says of sloth that it is "the poisoning of the will which extends to the refusal of joy and culminates in morbid introspection and despair."[71] While *acedia* and *tristitia* are archaic words, I fear "joy" may replace them as the forgotten word in some gray November future.

This is why this book doesn't matter. A person can learn every sin, know every truth, but where sloth is, there is no will to fight, to flee, to change. Sloth doesn't get up and run, nor does it dance; sloth permits no vulnerability, and accountability becomes just too heavy a burden to expect anyone to carry, so why bother? With sloth, we lie down so as to rot more comfortably.

Hebrews spends some time on sloth. In chapter 5, we encounter the beginning of a bookended section that begins: "We have much to say about this, but it is hard to make it clear to you because you no longer try to understand" (v. 11). That last part—"you no longer try to understand"—is the word that opens and closes this brief section on sloth. We read it as someone no longer trying to understand, but we could just as well substitute the word lazy or sluggish or slothful. Said another way, "We could tell you all about this, but why waste our time? You've quit."

Rather than actually giving up, though, the writer goes on:

> *In fact, though by this time you ought to be teachers, you need someone to teach you the elementary truths of God's word all over again. You need milk, not solid food! Anyone who lives on milk, being still an infant, is not acquainted with the teaching about righteousness. But solid food is for the mature, who by constant use have trained themselves to distinguish good from evil* (vv. 12–14).

These verses are pleading with the reader—with you—to acknowledge your legs. *You are not a slug!* it is saying, even if you are displaying some slug-like tendencies when it comes to faith. When we examined gluttony, we saw people who wanted Jesus to feed their bodies so they wouldn't have to work for food. Charles Spurgeon comments on this scene: "The incident is symbolic of the tendency to repose which is inherent in human nature, but if this desire were satisfied it would be the destruction of all character."[72] In other words, it is unhealthy to stay on the bottle. Spirituality is not intended to be an IV drip. When we don't eat spiritually, our character atrophies, withers, and dies. We exist as bodies, but we were made as souls with bodies. So we must feed our souls, too. For the Christian, this means sharing and teaching and contending and discerning.

Most of us, however, content ourselves with a passive faith. As you read this sentence, reflect on the last time you shared your faith—like, really shared it. For many of us, we have to go back some ways if we can think of a time at all. The reason for this is that we've subsisted on milk, and those milk meals haven't developed our strength of courage or wisdom. We have not built the muscle of love.

Early in faith, for many, we feel a high. Faith is like some drug, filling and intoxicating us. It is like falling in love for the first time when every thought but the beloved becomes peripheral. "I only have eyes for you," our soul sings to Jesus. And others hear us. In those early days, we share our faith. I used to work in college ministry. A huge challenge was keeping the kids in college for four years. They'd want to bolt to Thailand or Papua New Guinea, dead-set on some ends-of-the-earth mission for Christ.

Then come the middle years, when life kicks up. These years are long and hard. We echo the famous children's book, *Are You There, God? It's Me, Matt.* One day, after the high of initial faith wears off, we look around and find sin still slinking around—the body still rings. We thought we were done with temptation and lust and lies. Then, even worse, we begin to answer that ringing phone. Discouraged by our weakness, we turn to shame. Embarrassed by our shame, we hide, isolating ourselves into a spiritual existence that looks and feels more like a masquerade rather than the vibrant spiritual life that has been won for us. It is like being on a bad baseball team. I was on one once—many times, actually. Perhaps I was the problem all along! This one season in college was particularly brutal. It was apparent from our opening weekend that we were not very good. But some human tendency for honor and resilience thrummed to the surface—we fought! Yet we kept right on losing despite our momentary heroic denial. Then discouragement redoubled. Playing a game we loved turned into just running out the string on the season. By the end, none of us loved baseball quite the same way anymore. In truth, we probably hated it some for the cruelness of it—we listened, we played hard, we honored the game—all the things! Why did it bring defeat upon defeat?

And then these middle years concede into the later years of acedia. Our journeys—our lives—become like an oven on warm evermore.

This is the make-up of unhealthy churches. Churches that cannot grow spiritually. Churches without fruit. It is not the lost folks dragging things down. Nor is it the seekers. It is the roomful of self-professing, longtime believers who have become complacent. They've settled for spiritual languishing. A faith that, to use *The Simpsons* jargon, is more "meh" than meaningful. Passion has dried up, leaving us with a lackluster spirituality that ebbs and flows on the quality of the weekly sermon. This is sloth, and it keeps us from what God has for us.

The author of Hebrews then lays out some specific ways that sloth puts our souls to sleep:

> *Therefore let us move beyond the elementary teaching about Christ and be taken forward to maturity, not laying again the foundation of repentance from acts that lead to death, and of faith in God, instruction about cleansing rites, the laying on of hands, the resurrection of the dead, and eternal judgment.* (Hebrews 6:1–2)

The first on the author's list is "not laying the foundation of repentance from acts that lead to death." I recall working for a church where this one congregant would come down to the altar every single week at the end of the service. There, he would lay, weeping, tormented over his sin for the week. This level of penitent humility would have been admirable had it not been the exact same sin every single week. For years. I think what Hebrews would say to that guy is, "Bro, quit sluggin' around! Take up your mat and walk!" So many of us are content to let lust, pride, or anger just live rent-free in our hearts. We make them comfortable. Get them a drink. I heard a believer the other day talking about the best way to get drunk and avoid a severe hangover.

Hebrews would say, "When you gonna quit that foolishness? When you are forty? Fifty? How much life are you willing to surrender to sin?" Or think about greed and the Christian aptitude to make the poor in our lives, to make the church we attend, grovel for our money. We hold them hostage—*I'll give when you show progress* or *when you play the praise set I like.* Churches have to remind congregants that there are buckets in the back for their giving, like, every week. When was the last time a church made this announcement: "Hey, everyone. Stop! Please stop your giving for a few weeks. Give it elsewhere. We have too much money! Too many provisions. There is not enough room in the storehouses to contain your generosity!" The answer, I think, would be never. That never happens.

I halfway share a view with William James that, mostly, people stop changing. So, the person who is cynical in their twenties is unlikely to become hopeful in their thirties. By their forties, you had better get out of going to a movie or to dinner with that person at all costs. In old age, just forget about it. Or, more practically evident, again take the alcoholic. The longer a person is an alcoholic, the more of an alcoholic they become—the alcohol has a firmer grasp on their physical and emotional needs. Which also means that the longer someone is an alcoholic, the harder it is to quit. Spiritually, I think it operates the same way. If you descend the depths enough into darkness, eventually, the hill becomes just too steep to overcome or the darkness too opaque, and the muck and mire becomes our primary residence—we go from home to hovel.

We must fight. Then, in Christ, we overcome. Then we move on to the next boss. My son and I play video games together, and it works the same way. We don't defeat a foe and then decide the next night to backtrack to face him again. No, we press on to take hold of new terrain, to claim new lands.

Second on this list of sluggishness is our "faith in God." Many of us get cozy atop the fences of faith. We try to play spiritual Twister, with one foot planted on the red circle of the blood of Christ while the other foot is firmly planted on the pattern of this world. Think of the things that ratchet up our doubts? It might be the great fish in Jonah or the virgin birth. We wrestle with these things. But the thing about wrestling matches is that they have endings and victors. At some point, faith must win out in the arenas of doubt in our lives. Too often, we are content to date Jesus. Or we are willing to get engaged to appease pushy family members, but we are like one of those couples who is perpetually engaged. What the Bible is telling us here is that we need to commit. Christians ought not constantly be returning to the same tired controversies and halfhearted commitments. We are to follow Jesus every day, not just when convenient. We are to go all in and burn the boats in the various shores of our faith, not pull out an inflatable and float and drift. The adventure of faith is a swift-flowing river, not a shallow pool.

Third, the author of Hebrews mentions "rituals and preferences." Every age of Christians acts like disagreements about baptism and communion are novel. We love to debate them like we are the first ones on earth to have thought to do so—like the church fathers spent all their time training the ushers and greeters and making sure there was a special gift for visitors that isn't really a gift at all but rather a not-so-subtle marketing scheme. (Like, seriously, if I were to plant a church, I'd love for the special gift for new people to be a drone or PlayStation or something cool someone would actually want instead of a mug filled with cross-shaped potpourri and a list of mandatory membership classes.) We have debates within the faith, and this is fine. It is even important. But these differences of doctrine and opinion are seldom ultimate because these differences usually aren't directly about the person and work of Jesus. We spend a primary amount of time squabbling about secondary issues when what ought to be our first love is standing there neglected. And, what's worse, we spend even more time on tertiary issues that don't even rise to secondary status! I'm not sure about coffee and church. Let's really get good and distracted with a long-form series of posts and talks discussing it. Or how about drums! Might as well replace the drums with a dead horse for the beating they've gotten the last handful of decades. Christians have been given a world-saving mission, yet we are more concerned with how long we should have to stand during the weekly pretend-to-sing time. Hebrews here is calling us out of this distracted form of sluggishness and urging us to refocus on and through the cross of Jesus.

Fourth, the author lists the end times. Not a year goes by that I don't get a rather depictive mailer about the precise way the end times will look in watercolor imagery with an invite to hear some "expert" speak on the matter. Why do I need the talk when the picture says a millennium of words? If I start a church and advertise a series on Galatians, we won't even need the entirety of my basement to fit everyone. Not all the members of my own family will come downstairs for church that first week. But if we talk about the Tribulation—look out! We love to study our Bibles, especially if that study prevents us from actually having to live out what those Bibles clearly say. For many Christians, we'd rather sit and argue about how Jesus returns than live like he actually will. And this keeps us from growth—it creates spiritual sloth.

Truth is, we get saved—or pretend it—and we just run out the string. *Pilgrim's Progress* has a scene with a huge hill. The character is running up it. Then he walks. Next, he crawls. Finally, he camps. Camp becomes home if someone stays there. This is the state of spiritual sloth.

We grow lazy. Content with our apathy, we then wonder at the low-level thrum of sadness in our lives and in our churches. It is no wonder that the walls don't shake from worship. It is no wonder that we don't bound out into the world to take on the week. It is no wonder that mountains don't move in our lives. It is no wonder because, in sloth, there is no wonder at all. This is a jarring statement unless, of course, sloth is alive, in which case we skim on with a yawn.

Hebrews, however, blares on like a foghorn of wakefulness:

> *It is impossible for those who have once been enlightened, who have tasted the heavenly gift, who have shared in the Holy Spirit, who have tasted the goodness of the word of God and the powers of the coming age and who have fallen away, to be brought back to repentance. To their loss they are crucifying the Son of God all over again and subjecting him to public disgrace (6:4–6).*

That passage could be saying all sorts of things. On the surface, it reads like it is saying someone could be at risk of losing their salvation. That doesn't square with biblical teaching since there is nothing we did to earn our salvation. It would be troubling if there then was a work more powerful than the salvific work of Christ on our behalf.

It could, then, be referencing a false salvation. This would be reminiscent of Jesus's warning in Matthew 7 in which a religious person is turned away from God with the tragic words, "Depart from me. I never knew you." What this would mean is that a person might have some of the experiences of the faith—they sense God's power and even feel his enlightenment in some profound ways—without submitting to a full identity in the faith. It is like gaining some of the benefits of a relationship without committing to a marriage.

A third option—and the one I think gets to the heart of things— is that the author is appealing to the amygdala of a believer, the almond-shaped part of the brain that keeps us alive. The amygdala activates when we are faced with an emergency. If the building you are in right now catches fire, you will not say, "Maybe I'll evacuate after this chapter. Matt is absolutely crushing this sloth stuff." No, the amygdala will have you dash from the building because it will sound the alarm to your body that your very life is on the line. That is what Hebrews is doing here.

My son had a period of night terrors. These were more than dreams. He'd be locked in writhing struggles, and my voice alone couldn't wake him from his torment. I'd have to physically take his head and torso in my hands and, lovingly, jam him down into his pillow a few times. Basically, I'd have to carefully, yet firmly, shake him awake. Spiritually, this passage is shaking us: *Wake up!* It is calling the Christian to care, to fight, to bleed, to pant for Christ, to actually love God, and to follow Christ in a full, lavish, risky, spontaneous, open, complete, rapturous way.

In the story of the Prodigal Son, the boy ends up broke and at the pig pen. Then he is *in* the pig pen. Then he is eating the pig slop. He is on his belly—a picture of sloth. Dorothy Sayers says of sloth that it is "the sin that believes nothing, cares for nothing, seeks to know nothing, interferes with nothing, enjoys nothing, lives for nothing, and remains alive only because there is nothing it would die for."[73] Or, in the words of Hebrews 6:7–8:

> *Land that drinks in the rain often falling on it and that produces a crop useful to those for whom it is farmed receives the blessing of God. But land that produces thorns and thistles is worthless and is in danger of being cursed. In the end it will be burned.*

Sloth makes us less than human. It makes us worthless, crawling around and scrounging at the scraps.

Now, some people avoid dealing with sloth because of their morality. But all this usually means is that they lack courage. Many people are moral only because they are too scared or tired or lazy to sin in overt, creative fashion, not necessarily because they are trusting Jesus. Many a church is filled with moral people who aren't actually functionally righteous, but rather they are stewards of souls made too timid to get up from their spiritual stupor and try in either direction—to be either bad or good.

The Prodigal doesn't become a pig, though, does he? He dreams still; he hopes on. And he gets up. Goes home. Runs to his father. I wonder if you'd be so brave even today?

Part of the reason I think Hebrews is attempting to jar believers awake is the language of verse 9: *Even though we speak like this, dear friends, we are convinced of better things in your case—the things that have to do with salvation.* There is another way. It is showing the worst-case scenario—it is pointing out the pig pen, but then it is handing us a map home. It goes on:

> *God is not unjust; he will not forget your work and the love you have shown him as you have helped his people and continue to help them. We want each of you to show this same diligence to the very end, so that what you hope for may be fully realized. We do not want you to become lazy, but to imitate those who through faith and patience inherit what has been promised.* (Hebrews 6:9–12)

The path home is in diligence. We arrive nowhere by becoming no one, by lying in the mud and waiting. Rather, we sprint toward what God has for us. We run like hell and heaven, and eternity—like flourishing—hangs in the cosmic balance.

Our soul was not made for dislocation. It has a place, a function, and a blessed form. It was redeemed to relocation. God desires our souls to live and move and inhale a deep joy of desire. Brooks says this of desire:

> *Desire makes you adhesive. Desire pushes you to get close—to the person, job, or town you love. But lack of desire makes*

you detached, and instills in you over time an attitude of emotional avoidance, a phony nonchalance.

He goes on to quote Danish novelist, Matias Dalsgaard, in referencing the desire-less person:

> *Such a person must have no stable or solid foundation to build upon, and yet nonetheless tries to build his way out of his problem. It's an impossible situation. You can't compensate for having a foundation made of quicksand by building a new story on top. But this person takes no notice and hopes that the problem down in the foundation won't be found out if only the construction work on the top keeps going.*[74]

By God's Spirit, we need a desire that plunges the depths, that doesn't settle for half-measures and shortcuts. Sin's ultimate win is when we don't allow the gardener to get down to the roots. A renewed desire for God allows us to dig to the depths, forever and more.

AFTERWORD

O, how is the world darkened, clouded, distracted, and torn to pieces by those dreadful enemies of mankind called words!
—Jonathan Edwards

THE ABOVE QUOTE comes from a man whose supreme gift was communication. My ability is much more limited than his; my own words, more adversarial still. And yet I press on. You see, I know what I don't know. Perhaps it is what I'm most certain of. I'm certain my words fail, my theological understanding falls far short, and my manner and style leave one darkened, clouded, distracted, and torn to pieces. But I do know this: It is raining.

From where I scratch out these labored sentences, I watch a late summer storm swirl beyond the windowpane. The trees dance—or is that more of a quaking? The earth gulps the water, famished after a long, dry summer. The water cools the earth, the air. Fall is coming.

My words may fail in this book—for some readers, that is a certainty. But for the Christian, the failure is in living a tepid, worldly life, for settling. It is gazing out the window, like I'm doing now, only beyond that window lie vast forests approaching splendid mountains—purer vistas and rollicking adventures woo sweetly like some heavenly whisper. We ought to throw off every hindrance and run toward those rolling hills and scenic views. We, along the way, should meet and make friends, made merry with the camaraderie that comes from striking off together toward a better beyond. Exhilaration should fill us as life becomes ever nearer to what it was intended to be.

But instead, we sit. From time to time, we stare with longing at all that awaits us out that window of glory. Eventually, though, even those stolen gazes feel like too much work or conjure up too much fear or awaken too deep a longing, so we close the shades to possibilities, and we sit. Darkened. Clouded. Distracted. We are torn to pieces by the life we choose, abandoning the life chosen for us and the great Chooser Himself. We go on sitting till we die—only by that point there is scarcely a difference between these two wretched unrealities—the sitting and the dying look so much the same.

My words fail, and many of our efforts will too, but our God is good. In James, after coaxing the Christian to choose true wisdom over false wisdom and before laying out that path as the way of humility over pride, the author reminds us that God "gives us more grace" (4:6).

Yes, when we join our efforts to his power, he will lift us up. In him, we will move and breathe and have our being. We will leave the spiritual wasteland and strike off. We will explore the vastness of his wilderness freedom, running without growing weary. Filled by this Spirit, we will resist the devil, and he will flee. And with steadiness—the very beating of the heart—will come the mind, body, and soul realization that we are invited by a good Father to "draw near to me."

Fall is coming. And my words fail. But winter gives way to spring. Each year, it happens. Life abundant awaits.

ENDNOTES

1   John Rotelle et al., *The Works of Saint Augustine* (New City Press, 2012).

2   C. S. Lewis, *Mere Christianity* (HarperCollins Publishers, 1952).

3   C. S. Lewis, *The Weight of Glory and Other Addresses* (William Collins, 2013).

4   Jonathan Edwards, *Sinners in the Hands of an Angry God and Other Puritan Sermons* (Dover Publications, 2005).

5   John Owen, *The Mortification of Sin: A Puritan's View of How to Deal with Sin in Your Life* (Christian Heritage, 2006).

6   Psalm 34:8.

7   Sayers uses this construct concerning societies. Lewis also employs the framework—especially in *The Screwtape Letters*. I think I first heard the sentiment in a sermon by a pastor named Dan Greene, who probably doesn't have much earthly fame but is well-regarded in eternity.

8   Brian G. Hedges, *Hit List: Taking Aim at the Seven Deadly Sins* (Cruciform Press, 2014).

9 Dante Alighieri and Dorothy L. Sayers, *The Divine Comedy, Part 2: Purgatory* (Penguin Classics, 1955).

10 Chesterton uses the phrasing a "fiercer delight" in *Orthodoxy*. The sentence and context escapes me, but it was a little three-word turn of phrase that made me want to write a thousand words just to have that title. More so, I'd like that life pursuit. To live a life constantly striving for a "fiercer delight."

11 C. S. Lewis, *Mere Christianity* (HarperCollins Publishers, 1952), 121–128.

12 Thomas Aquinas, John Milton, and Augustine, to name a few.

13 Around the time of release or Episodes I–III, this claim was widely asserted across fan sites, along with more critical sources like books and articles. One theological perspective was mentioned in Mike Cosper's book: *The Stories We Tell: How TV and Movies Long for and Echo Truth*.

14 Genesis 3:1.

15 Genesis 3:2–3.

16 Genesis 3:4–5.

17 Genesis 3:6.

18 C. S. Lewis, *The Lion, the Witch, and the Wardrobe* (HarperCollins, 2018).

19 David M. Morens, "Death of a President," *New England Journal of Medicine*, 341, no. 24 (December 9, 1999): 1845–1850, https://doi.org/10.1056/nejm199912093412413.

20 William Ernest Henley, "Invictus," *Poetry Foundation*, 1875, www.poetryfoundation.org/poems/51642/invictus.

21 Isbel Best, *The Collected Sermons of Dietrich Bonhoeffer* (Fortress Press, 2012).

22 Mitch Hedberg used this joke (and style) often throughout his stand-up career from 1990 to 2005.

23 John Piper, "How Do I Kill My Pride?" Desiring God, June 3, 2019, www.desiringgod.org/interviews/how-do-i-kill-my-pride.

24 David Brooks, *The Road to Character* (Random House, 2016).

25 Jenny-Lyn de Klerk, "Augustine on Humility," The Gospel Coalition, 2023, ca.thegospelcoalition.org/article/augustine-on-humility/.

26 Genesis 3:19.

27 Aesopus, et al., *Aesop's Fables* (Wordsworth Classics, 1995).

28 Plato, et al., *Gorgias: Revised Edition* (Penguin, 2004).

29 Robert H. Frank and Philip J Cook, *The Winner-Take-All Society: Why the Few at the Top Get so Much More Than the Rest of Us* (Virgin Books, 2010).

30 Daniel Kahneman, *Thinking, Fast and Slow* (Farrar, Straus and Giroux, 2011).

31 Dan Ariely, *The (Honest) Truth about Dishonesty: How We Lie to Everyone—Especially Ourselves* (Harper Perennial, 2013).

32 Richard E. Nisbett, *The Geography of Thought: How Asians and Westerners Think Differently—and Why* (Nicholas Brealey, 2011).

33 Dorothy Leigh Sayers, *The Mind of the Maker* (Harper San Francisco, 1970).

34 Aristotle and C. D. C. Reeve, *Rhetoric* (Hackett Publishing Company, Inc, 2018), book II, chapter 9.

35 Buechner, Frederick. *Wishful Thinking: A Theological ABC* (Collins, 1973).

36 Edward Erwin, *The Freud Encyclopedia* (Routledge, 2003).

37 Richard Allen Epstein, *Simple Rules for a Complex World* (Harvard University Press, 1995).

38 Jonathan Edwards, *The Nature of True Virtue* (University of Michigan Press, 1960).

39 *The Office*, season 1, episode 5, "Basketball," written by Greg Daniels and Mindy Kaling.

40 David Greenfield, "Facebook Envy: How Social Media Can Lead to Depression," HuffPost, July 11, 2011.

41 David Riesman, *The Lonely Crowd* (Yale University Press, 1989).

42 Mark 12:17.

43 Keith James Holyoak and Robert G Morrison, *The Cambridge Handbook of Thinking and Reasoning* (Cambridge University Press, 2011).

44 Psalm 139:23–24.

45 Allan D. Fitzgerald, *Augustine Through the Age* (Wm. B. Eerdmans Publishing, April 9, 2009).

46 John 10:30.

47 Anne Lamott and Anchor Books, *Traveling Mercies: Some Thoughts on Faith* (Anchor Books, 2006).

48 C. S. Lewis, *The Weight of Glory and Other Addresses* (William Collins, 2013).

49 Charles Harold Dodd, *The Parables of the Kingdom* (MacMillan Publishing Company, 1961).

50 Ecclesiastes 3:11.

51 Michael K. Williams, "The Million-Dollar Rehab: Inside America's Most Luxurious Addiction Treatment," *The Atlantic*, 2019; Rachel Aviv, "Luxury Rehab: The Pros and Cons of High-End Addiction Treatment," *The New Yorker*, August 8, 2021.

52 Paul Israel, *Edison: A Life of Invention* (John Wiley & Sons, 2000).

53 Matthew 6:24.

54 Mark 12:41–44.

55 There has been much researched and written about the softening sex ethic of the West. Here's an article to begin your rabbit-hole dive if so inclined: Mary Bowerman, "Survey: Sleeping Together Before a First Date is A-OK, But Cracked Phones Are a Put Off," *USA Today*, February 6, 2017.

56 C. S. Lewis, *The Four Loves* (Harperone, 1960).

57 Carell said this while presenting the award for Best Sound Editing during the 2018 Academy Awards.

58 Augustine and R. S. Pine-Coffin, *Confessions of Saint Augustine* (Penguin Books, 2004), book VIII.

59 This quote is attributed to Twain and his 1897 book "Following the Equator." I came across it, however, online in a reddit thread of all places. There it can be found as the handwritten caption on an iconic picture of Twain aboard a ship. He, presumably, signed his name, and then someone below this wrote in "Clemens." In the picture he is alone. Whether he is "good" or not, I cannot say.

60 Romans 7:15.

61 2 Corinthians 10:5.

62 Mark Twain, *The Wit and Wisdom of Mark Twain: A Book of Quotations* (Dover Publications, Inc, 1999).

63 C. S. Lewis, *The Weight of Glory and Other Addresses* (William Collins, 2013).

64 Charles Dickens, *Oliver Twist* (Oxford University Press, 2008).

65 This is in Aquinas's *Summa Theologica*. Here is an accessible collection of many of those ideas: Thomas Aquinas and Ralph McInerney, *Thomas Aquinas: Selected Works* (Penguin Books, 1998).

66 Articles and studies on nostalgia are plentiful. Here are a couple: Troy Allen, "The Branding Power of Nostalgia: Where It Can Take You," *Forbes*, January 27, 2023; Arthur Brooks, "Nostalgia Is a Shield Against Unhappiness," *The Atlantic*, March 9, 2023.

67 C. S. Lewis, *The Lion, the Witch, and the Wardrobe* (HarperCollins, 2018).

68 Malcolm Gladwell, host, *Revisionist History*, podcast, "The Magic Wand Experiment," Thursday, June 30, 2022. https://www.youtube.com/watch?v=HxXPjz40Kcw.

69 William R. Cook and Ronald B. Herzman, *The Medieval Book of Vices and Virtues: The Seven Deadly Sins and the Seven Virtues* (Oxford University Press, 2003).

70 David Brooks, *The Second Mountain: The Quest for a Moral Life* (Random House, 2020).

71 Dorothy L. Sayers et al., *The Gospel in Dorothy L. Sayers: Selections from Her Novels, Plays, Letters, and Essays.* (Plough Publishing House, 2018).
72 Charles Spurgeon, *12 Sermons on Repentance* (Baker Books, 1977).
73 Dorothy Leigh Sayers, *Creed or Chaos?* (Sophia Inst Press, 1995).
74 David Brooks, *The Second Mountain: The Quest for a Moral Life* (Random House, 2020).